The Historical Series of the Reformed Church
in America

No. 13

TWO CENTURIES PLUS:

The Story of New Brunswick Seminary

by

Howard G. Hageman

With Chapter 13 by
Benjamin Alicea

Wm. B. Eerdmans Publishing Co.
Grand Rapids, Michigan

Copyright © 1984 by Wm. B. Eerdmans Publishing Company
255 Jefferson S.E., Grand Rapids, MI 49503

Library of Congress Cataloging in Publication Data

Hageman, Howard G., 1921-
  Two centuries plus.

  (The Historical series of the Reformed Church in
America; no. 13)
  Includes bibliographical references.
  1. New Brunswick Theological Seminary—History.
I. Alicea, Benjamin, 1952-   II. Title.   III. Title:
2 centuries plus. IV. Series.
BV4070.N36H34   1984   207'.74942   84-10776
ISBN 0-8029-0039-4

Contents

DEDICATION

To all those who have studied at New Brunswick Seminary and think of it as their alma mater.

Illustrations

The Historical Series of the Reformed Church in America

This series has been inaugurated by the General Synod of the Reformed Church in America, acting through its Commission on History, for the purpose of encouraging historical research and providing a medium wherein this knowledge may be shared with the academic community and with the members of the denomination in order that a knowledge of the past may contribute to right action in the present.

It is an especial pleasure to present to the church this volume to celebrate the bicentennial of New Brunswick Theological Seminary in the Year of our Lord 1984.

General Editor

The Rev. Donald J. Bruggink, Ph.D., Western Theological Seminary

The Commission on History

The Rev. John Arnone, Ph.D., Monmouth College
Barbara Frierson, Oakland, California
The Rev. Norman J. Kansfield, Ph.D., Colgate Rochester Divinity School
Cornelia B. Kennedy, Northwestern College
The Rev. Joseph A. Loux, Jr., Helderberg Reformed Church
The Rev. Edwin G. Mulder, D.D., General Secretary, RCA
The Rev. Dennis Voskuil, Ph.D., Hope College

Preface

When New Brunswick Seminary celebrated its centennial in 1884 a large volume was published containing not only all of the addresses delivered at the celebration, but a detailed and scholarly history of the first 100 years as well. For the story of 200 years I have relied heavily on that history, but I have chosen to approach it in a different way. I have tried to write this book not for the technical historian of theological education, but for the person interested in learning more about the oldest venture in the field in this country. Footnotes have been kept to a minimum in the hope that what is in these pages will read more like a narrative than a historical reference book.

The claim of New Brunswick Seminary to be the oldest Protestant theological seminary in North America has often been disputed because the school did not move to New Brunswick to become a residential institution until 1810. From 1784 until that time it had only a part-time faculty, and classes were held in a variety of places, most often in faculty homes. In spite of this, since the authorization for the school in 1784 clearly required that those studying with the designated professors must already have a college degree, there is ample justification for claiming that New Brunswick is indeed the oldest theological seminary in the country.

I

Foreshadowings of Things To Come

Peter Henry Dorsius was a man who had come to this country with a dual sense of mission. Perhaps there was nothing so surprising in that since in his own person he represented two different traditions. A native of Germany, he had come to the University of Groningen in the Netherlands for his theological education, which he completed in Leiden in 1737.

Sometime before Dorsius's graduation, the Classis of Amsterdam had received a request from the consistory of a small Dutch Reformed congregation in Bucks County, Pennsylvania, for a domine to be sent to them. Although the church had been in existence since 1710, only in recent years had it become able financially to support a minister. The classis was interested in the request not only because it was responsible for providing ministers to the North American churches, but also because it had become increasingly aware of the large number of Palatine Germans, many of them members of the Reformed Church, who had been flooding into Pennsylvania. Charged with responsibility for the congregations in New York and New Jersey for more than a century, the Classis of Amsterdam wondered what its responsibilities for churches in Pennsylvania should be.

The request from the Bucks County consistory seemed to provide a possible way of finding out. Here was a Dutch congregation in the midst of a rising German area. If someone could be found for the Bucks County congregation, who also had some familiarity with German traditions and the German language, that person could provide reliable information for the classis to help it in determining its new responsibilities. The committee of the classis must have been delighted to discover among those completing

1

their theological studies a young German named Peter Henry
Dorsius.

Almost immediately the classis was in touch both with Dorsius
and with the Bucks County consistory. Dorsius agreed to take on
the task in Pennsylvania. Since the consistory had sent money for
a new domine's travel expenses, the classis asked whether some
of that money could be devoted to tuition fees, since the young
candidate had not yet finished his studies. Arrangements satisfactory to all were worked out and the new domine, after he was
ordained in Groningen on May 29, 1737, set sail for Philadelphia
on July 11 and arrived on October 5. Dorsius was asked by the
classis to provide all the information he could about the situation
of the German Reformed in Pennsylvania, as well as to minister
to the Dutch Reformed people of Bucks County.

The story of the way in which Dorsius fulfilled his duties is one
that does not concern us here. It may be worth noting, however,
that of all the domines in the New World who had difficulties
with ecclesiastical authority in the Netherlands, he was the only
one who took the time and the trouble to travel back to the
Netherlands, meeting personally with classis and synod in an
attempt to straighten out the misunderstandings.

One of the problems which Dorsius saw soon after his arrival
in Pennsylvania was the lack of a trained ministry and the way
in which that prevented the growth of the church. From the
Dutch point of view, that training had to involve several years of
study in the theological faculty of a university. Since no universities of that kind existed in North America, the only solution was
to send the candidates to the Netherlands for their education and
ordination, a procedure which was both cumbersome and
expensive.

Such requirements put both the Dutch and the German Reformed churches at a disadvantage with their Congregational and
Presbyterian neighbors, whose candidates were required only to
attend a college, such as Harvard or Yale (or later Princeton), and
after graduation to become apprenticed to a local pastor. To the

fathers in the Netherlands a local pastor was not an adequate substitute for a group of university professors.

For Peter Dorsius the problem was symbolized by the strange case of John Henry Goetschius, the son of a Swiss Reformed pastor who, after some vicissitudes at home, had come to Philadelphia in 1735 to be pastor of the German Reformed Church there. Poor Pastor Goetschius died within an hour or so after landing in Philadelphia, leaving a family of eight children of whom John Henry, at eighteen, was the oldest. Since he had had some preliminary training for the ministry in Zurich, to support his family he did the only thing he knew: he began preaching in the numerous German Reformed congregations in Pennsylvania which were without a minister. Because of his innate abilities, John Henry Goetschius was very well received.

Apparently Goetschius was aware of the anomaly of his situation because in the spring of 1737 he applied to the Presbyterian Synod of Philadelphia for ordination. After carefully examining him and his testimonials, on May 27 the synod came to the following conclusion.

> . . . though he [Goetschius] appeared well skilled in the learned languages [the result of his training in Zurich, *ed.*], yet inasmuch as they found him altogether ignorant in college learning and but poorly read in divinity, his ordination to the ministry must at present be deferred. And therefore for his better instruction [they] advise him, being willing to encourage him, to put himself under the tuition and care of some minister for competent time that he may be better accomplished for the work he is engaged in.[1]

The synod did allow him to preach occasionally to German Reformed congregations because of their "necessitous condition," but that was the extent of its encouragement.

There can be little doubt that, because of his concern for the German Reformed congregations in eastern Pennsylvania, Dorsius became aware of the Goetschius problem soon after his arrival in Bucks County. Here was a competent and enthusiastic young man, desperately needed in this situation. If he was, however, refused ordination by American Presbyterians, what would happen to him if he applied to Holland? The Synod of South Holland had now taken charge of German Reformed affairs in Pennsylvania and seems to have been somewhat more relaxed in its views than its counterpart in Amsterdam. It urged Goetschius to follow Presbyterian advice: discontinue his ministry and seek further training with a pastor. This would lead, hopefully, to a regular ordination in the New World.

It is impossible to say whether it was at the urging of the Synod of South Holland or on his own personal initiative, but the fact is that late in 1738 or early in 1739 Dorsius invited John Henry Goetschius to move into the parsonage in Southampton, Bucks County. In exchange for assisting the domine, he was to receive the theological training necessary to fit him for the ministry. In and of itself such an arrangement might not have been too unusual, but in that time and situation word apparently traveled rapidly.

The great leader of the evangelical forces of the Dutch Reformed Church in America at this time was Theodorus Jacobus Frelinghuysen, minister at the Raritan. Having heard of the theological tutorial which was beginning in Bucks County, Frelinghuysen sent his son John to the Pennsylvania instructor. John was very young at the time and was to receive further training in the Netherlands, but his father's enthusiasm for the Bucks County experiment is clear from the following testimonial dated April 14, 1740:

> As we are obliged to defend the good name of our neighbor and brother, especially when assailed by evil tongues and pens; therefore, I consider myself in duty bound to give the following testimony concerning our dear colleague, Rev. P. H. Dorsius, minister of Jesus Christ in his church in Bucks County, Pennsylvania, as follows.
>
> That beside a general interchange of letters, I have had much conversation and general intercourse with his reverence greatly to my comfort and edification: and that as an eye witness of his doings and hearer of his words, I am constrained in love to give my judgment

that said Rev. Domine Dorsius is a learned, gifted, graciously endowed and faithful minister and whose services have not remained
without a blessing.

I have therefore gladly committed and entrusted one of my sons,
Johannes by name, to the instruction and tuition of his reverence.
He also has his lodgings and his board with him. It is also possible
that our oldest son, Theodore, who has already studied Latin under
Domine van Sandvoord for some years will soon be sent to his rev-
erence for instruction.[2]

It is not known whether Theodore was the second Frelinghuysen to study with Dorsius or whether it was his brother
Henricus. We do know from a letter written by Flatbush domine
Bernardus Freeman to the Classis of Amsterdam on April 23,
1741, that at that time Dorsius had two of Frelinghuysen's sons
under his tutelage. In the same letter Freeman claimed that the
Classis of Rotterdam had "authorized and empowered Dorsius to
qualify and ordain to the holy ministry persons of suitable endowments and piety, fitted to edify the church and called by the
same."[3]

Knowing the concern of the Classis of Rotterdam and the Synod
of South Holland for the spiritual welfare of the Germans in
Pennsylvania, it is not impossible to believe that Dorsius did have
some such mandate for the German churches, but it is more
likely that our Pennsylvania friend was very free in interpreting
the responsibility which had been given him. The fact remains,
however, that we have accounted for three of his students, and
Freeman claims that there were one or two others, not difficult
to identify. One was David Marinus, probably recommended to
Dorsius by Frelinghuysen, even though others doubtless shared
in his theological education. Another was Johannes Casparus
Fryenmoet, a pious young man from Zurich, who had come to
the New World as an indentured servant and settled in Port
Jervis, New York. Three congregations on the Delaware which
had been organized by the domine in Kingston and were served
by him felt that the time had come to secure their own minister
and that Fryenmoet was the person for the job. Having heard

that Dorsius was authorized to train ministerial candidates, the
consistories sent their choice to him and paid the tuition charges.

The case of Johathan Du Bois is somewhat less certain. Related
to a well-known family in the New Paltz area, Johathan lived in
southern New Jersey where he was educated as a Presbyterian.
After spending some time in the Presbyterian synod's school in
New London, Pennsylvania, he arrived in Southampton just at
the end of Dorsius's tenure there. Whether he studied with Dorsius or came to serve as his assistant (and after 1751 as his successor) is not clear. The same uncertainty also prevails in the case
of John Mauritius Goetschius, John Henry's younger brother.
The record says that Mauritius was prepared for the ministry by
his brother Henry, but a letter sent to Amsterdam in 1743 documents that on his trip to Holland Dorsius took both Mauritius
Goetschius and Theodore Frelinghuysen with him.[4] That fact
would seem to argue a close relationship arising from the
classroom.

Dorsius's career came to a tragic end. By 1749 he had become
an alcoholic, and his consistory suspended him from further service. By this time he had already returned to the Netherlands,
where he applied for further service overseas, but his record in
North America prevented that. Dorsius disappears from the record after 1750, though his wife whom he left in Pennsylvania
continued to be supported by the church in the Netherlands until
1776.

Peter Henry Dorsius surely deserves better recognition, in
spite of his unhappy end. His kitchen seminary in Bucks County,
with possibly as many as seven students, was certainly one of the
first of its kind in North America. The two Frelinghuysen boys
were licensed and ordained by the Classis of Amsterdam with
little or no further instruction, no small tribute to the thorough-
ness of Dorsius's tutelage. Fryenmoet, Marinus, Du Bois, and
Mauritius Goetschius were all useful ministers in the American
church, while John Henry Goetschius became one of its leaders.

More than that, with his kitchen seminary Dorsius set a pattern
which would increasingly be imitated in the American Dutch
Reformed Church. The success of Dorsius's protegés in both this

country and in the Netherlands led to questioning concerning
the necessity of Dutch training for ministerial candidates. The
acceptance earned by the six or seven graduates of Dorsius's
Bucks County school as they began to serve pastorates in the
American church caused a number of questions to arise concerning the entire traditional system of ministerial training.

Even before Dorsius's arrival in Pennsylvania, there had been
growing agitation in the American Reformed churches for some
kind of assembly with at least limited powers. The Classis of
Amsterdam seems to have vacillated on the question for a number
of years, but it finally granted permission for the formation of
such a body which was to be called a "coetus." The first meeting
of the coetus was held in September of 1747 in the consistory
room of the New York church. Its formation marked the beginning of a new era in the story of the Reformed Church in America.
Although the assembly had no real power and a report of its
proceedings had to be sent to Amsterdam for approval, it provided a forum for mutual discussion of American questions. One
can easily imagine that one of the most frequent topics of conversation was the need for American education and ordination,
in spite of the adamant stand taken by the fathers in Amsterdam.

It was at about the same time as the formation of the coetus
that the citizens of New York, disturbed that theirs was one of
the few colonies without an institution of higher learning, began
to take steps to remedy that situation. A series of lotteries was
held, beginning in 1746. By 1751 the lotteries had produced
almost 3,500 pounds. In that year the moneys were vested in ten
trustees, seven of whom were Episcopalians, two Dutch Reformed, and one Presbyterian. The predominance of Episcopalians caused alarm in some quarters, especially Presbyterian, that
the proposed college would be narrowly Episcopalian in its make-
up and not open to all.

These fears increased in 1754 when Trinity Church offered to
provide land for the college on condition that the president should
always be an Episcopalian and that the Anglican liturgy would be
used in all chapel services. In the ensuing battle to secure a
charter from the lieutenant governor and the New York assembly

on these terms, the support of the Dutch was essential since they were still the most numerous element in the population.

On October 25, 1754, the consistory of the New York church petitioned the assembly for the inclusion in the charter of a chair of Dutch Reformed divinity, implicitly making this the price of its support. But De Lancey, the lieutenant governor, was taking no chances on an assembly debate. In November he affixed his seal to the charter for a college which should be totally Episcopalian, even though it provided for minority representatives on the board of governors.

One of these representatives was Domine Johannes Ritzema, the senior minister of the New York church. At the first meeting, on May 7, 1755, he proposed to the Board of Governors that the inclusion of a chair of Dutch Reformed divinity might go far toward soothing some of the animosity which the charter of the college had aroused. Lieutenant Governor De Lancey indicated his willingness to accept such an amendment, with the result that at the meeting of June 3 an amendment was passed providing for the establishment of a "Professor of Divinity according to the doctrine, disciplines and worship established by the National Synod of Dort."

Ritzema's move, which was quickly disavowed by his consistory, had the result of placing the question of American theological education squarely before the Reformed Church. Had it succeeded, it would have meant that training for the ministry of the Reformed Church in America would have taken place in King's College (now Columbia University), an Anglican institution. David Demarest has put it succinctly.

> It was not to be expected that the Dutch Churches in the other parts of the country should favor a professorship which, though intended for the benefit of all, was yet to be filled by the Consistory of one congregation, though it was the Metropolitan Church, and to be under the control of a Board of Governors which was not in sympathy with the Dutch Church.[5]

Before the King's College controversy broke in 1754, there had been much discussion in the coetus about the need for an American Reformed college. Once word of Ritzema's plan was out, Theodore Frelinghuysen, probably one of Dorsius's old students and by now the minister of the important church in Albany, called a special meeting of the coetus which met in New York on May 30, 1755. The action taken at this meeting is worth quoting, at least in part.

> . . . We pastors and elders of the Reformed Church of both prov- inces, New York and New Jersey, in North America, being assembled in a Coetus and having established an alliance among ourselves, do resolve in these present critical times to strive with all our energy and in the fear of God, to plant a university or seminary for young men destined to study in the learned languages and in the liberal arts, and who are to be instructed in the philosophical sciences; also that it may be a school of the prophets in which young Levites and Nazarites of God may be prepared to enter upon the sacred minis- terial office in the church of God.[6]

The document was signed by twelve domines, four of whom had been students of Dorsius, while three others had studied with Dorsius's star pupil, John Henry Goetschius.

In a further, more far-reaching action, the coetus at this same meeting voted to assume all the powers of a classis, including qualifying men for the ministry and ordination. It further ap- pointed Theodore Frelinghuysen to visit the Netherlands to raise funds for the proposed college and seminary.

Needless to say, the action of the coetus horrified Ritzema and his friends and resulted in a genuine sundering of the denomi- nation. The larger group, still using the name coetus, though acting as a classis, pressed forward toward its goal of a completely independent American church, while the minority, calling itself the "conferentie," now that the King's College issue was a dead letter, sought to maintain the old ways and the traditional con- nections with the Netherlands. While each group had its rabid partisans, there were also many ministers and congregations who said "a plague on both your houses" and sought to continue in an independently neutral way.

Theodore Frelinghuysen's congregation in Albany was just such a group. Though it had no sympathy with Ritzema's attempt to place a chair of Dutch Reformed divinity in King's College, neither did it share its domine's enthusiasm for an American college. Recognizing the need of support from the two major congregations in North America (Albany and New York), Frelinghuysen spent the next few years trying to secure such support. His own congregation proved unsympathetic and the New York consistory refused to answer his letters. When in 1759 he felt increased resistance in the Albany congregation to his zealous evangelicalism, he resigned his pulpit and set sail for the Netherlands on October 10.

Frelinghuysen left with high expectations for the success of his mission because of the experience of Michael Schlatter who had visited the Netherlands in 1751 on behalf of the German Reformed churches of Pennsylvania. He had been royally welcomed and had raised approximately 12,000 pounds in Holland for the support of ministers and school teachers. By comparison, however, Frelinghuysen's mission was a failure. Had he gone soon after the coetus action of 1755, he might have been successful. By now, not only was the cause which he represented four years old, but the controversies of the American churches had spilled over into the Netherlands, and the Classis of Amsterdam was not sympathetic.

Domine Frelinghuysen remained in the Netherlands for two years, years which must have been a time of great frustration for him. Finally, after every door had been closed and all of his best efforts had proved fruitless, he set sail for home in 1761. The ship on which he was traveling made the crossing safely and anchored off Sandy Hook. While it was there, Frelinghuysen mysteriously fell from the deck and was drowned. No adequate explanation of the accident has ever been found, but at the time there was more than one suggestion that, because of the failure of his mission, his death was actually a suicide.

In the meantime efforts looking to the establishment of an American school were by no means discontinued at home. Since the leadership of the coetus was in New Jersey, it was in that colony that the push was the greatest. The leaders of the movement were John Henry Goetschius, now living in Hackensack, David Marinus of Passaic, Samuel Verbryck of Tappan, and John Leydt of New Brunswick. Goetschius and Marinus had been students of Dorsius, while Leydt and Verbryck had been trained by Goetschius and John Frelinghuysen. The influence of the Bucks County kitchen seminary is obvious!

The most stalwart supporter of the cause, however, was Jacob Rutsen Hardenbergh, a Kingston boy, who had been trained and ordained by the coetus in 1758. He spent the years from 1761 to 1763 in the Netherlands on personal business, the first American trained minister to visit the mother country. While it may be that he left a favorable impression which ultimately worked to the benefit of the American cause, his immediate report on his return to New Jersey was that the Classis of Amsterdam was still resolutely opposed to an American classis or an American college.

What might be called the New Jersey Reformed cabal kept asking successive governors for a charter for their school with no success, until on November 10, 1766, Governor William Franklin, the illegitimate son of Benjamin, yielded to the request. On that date he granted a charter for what was to be known as Queen's College. (Was there some irony in the choice of the name after the fiasco with Ritzema and King's College?) No copy of the charter exists today, and it seems largely to have been a piece of paper since nothing was done to implement it. It did however provoke Ritzema to write to Amsterdam in 1767, urging the classis to see that nothing of the kind envisioned in the charter should ever be allowed by the classis.

There were several reasons for the delay in implementing the charter of 1766. Quite apart from a lack of financial resources, the sponsors of the movement were not agreed as to the location of the proposed school. Goetschius wanted to see it as an extension of his academy in Hackensack; Leydt felt it belonged in New Brunswick which had lost the College of New Jersey to Princeton; Verbryck was convinced that it belonged in Tappan.

A still greater reason for the delay was what might be called the Princeton diversion. Just before Governor Franklin granted the 1766 charter, Domine De Ronde, one of the New York ministers, proposed to the Board of Trustees at Princeton, of which he was a member, that a chair of Dutch divinity be created in that school. It was Ritzema's King's College proposal all over again, but this time in a Presbyterian school, a fact which De Ronde thought should make it more palatable.

The trustees tabled the proposal but in the meantime the Classis of Amsterdam came up with something quite similar as its solution to the American problem. In a letter sent to both the coetus and the conferentie, the classis expressed its disapproval of the King's College scheme, but also tried to discourage the creation of an independent American school which it felt could not be successful because it could not gain the support of the whole church.

The only solution, in the opinion of the classis, was to create a Dutch theological professorate in association with the College of New Jersey at Princeton, essentially the same scheme as that proposed by De Ronde. It is worth noting that at the time the Classis of Amsterdam made its proposal, Dr. Witherspoon, the Princeton president, visiting in the Netherlands, had extensive conversations with church leaders. He also met with a student in Utrecht named John Henry Livingston who was so captivated by Dr. Witherspoon that he became an enthusiastic supporter of the idea of Dutch Reformed theological training at Princeton. While there is no evidence that Witherspoon originated the idea, certainly the favorable impression which he left on Dutch ecclesiastical authorities did nothing to harm it.

In this country, however, the proposal fell on deaf ears. The coetus, having gone thus far in its efforts for its own school, was not to be turned back. The idea was "pregnant with difficulties," it replied to the classis. Still fascinated with his King's College proposal (which remained in the charter), Ritzema and his friends in the conferentie said that a union with the "Scotch Presbyterian

Academy at Princeton" was every bit as bad as an independent
Dutch Reformed college.

Once again Governor Franklin yielded to the request of the
Jersey Dutch and granted a second charter to Queen's College
on March 20, 1770. The terms were not unlike those of the first,
but there was one difference affecting the question of theological
education. The trustees were to appoint a president who must
not only be a member of the Dutch Reformed Church but must
also serve as professor of divinity. After all, in the words of the
charter, Queen's College was to be "for the education of youth
in the learned languages, liberal and useful arts and sciences, and
especially in divinity; preparing them for the ministry and other
good offices."[7]

By 1771 the trustees had decided to locate Queen's College in
New Brunswick and had chosen Frederick Frelinghuysen, John's
son and a Princeton graduate, to serve as tutor. Quarters were
secured in the town, and Queen's College was underway.

The difficult question still to be faced was the selection of a
president and professor of divinity as the charter of 1770 required. It was in the same year that John Henry Livingston returned from Utrecht to become one of the ministers of the Church
in New York. He had brought back with him a plan of union to
reunite the warring factions of the Dutch Church, which he presented to a special meeting held in New York in 1771. Only that
part of the plan relating to theological education need concern us
here.

Articles 28 and 29 of the Plan of Union take up the subject of
the theological professorate. Among other things they stipulate
the following.

> That we provisionally choose one or two professors to teach Di-
> dactic, Polemic, Exegetic Theology etc. in accordance with the prin-
> ciples of the doctrine of our Dutch Reformed churches . . .
> Such Professor or Professors shall have no connection with any
> English Academy, but shall deliver lectures on theology in their own

houses to such students only as can by suitable testimonials make it
appear that they have carefully exercised themselves in the preparatory branches for two or three years at a college or academy under
the supervision of competent teachers in the languages, philosophy
etc.[8]

The adoption of the Plan of Union not only demolished any
possibility for theological instruction at King's College, but it was
equally devastating for Queen's as well. The Classis of Amsterdam
which had prepared the plan was letting both Ritzema and Goetschius know what it thought of their efforts!

What is significant, however, is the way in which the provisions
of the Plan of Union present theological education as what today
would be called a post-graduate course. Attendance at theological
lectures presumes a college course as a prerequisite. As has been
previously noted, theological education in America up to this
point had been a question of apprenticeship after college. Here
for the first time it is outlined as a second academic career. The
Plan of Union contains one of the earliest calls for graduate education known in North America.

The prohibition of any connection between the theological professorate and any "English academy" in no way disturbed King's
which had its own constituency anyway, but it posed a problem
for the trustees of Queen's who had counted on the Dutch theological professor for their first president, as their charter stipu-
lated. A strange game of buck-passing ensued. The trustees
appealed directly to the Classis of Amsterdam for advice. The
classis referred the question to the General Body in America
which its Plan of Union had created. The General Body, meeting
in Kingston in the fall of 1773, reversed its own constitution and
"after mature deliberation" came to the following conclusions.

1. Brunswick is the most suitable place for the Professor's residence
   because of the presence of Queens College.
2. No one is to be chosen for this office except by nomination by the

Classis of Amsterdam and ratification by the General Body. The office of Theological Professor is superior in rank to the presidency of Queens, though the same person will occupy both offices.

3. The General Body undertakes to increase the funds (4,000 pounds) now held by the Trustees so that a sufficient call may be made.[9]

The General Body also sent a letter to the Classis of Amsterdam explaining why it had changed its mind and now felt that this was the best possible plan under the circumstances. The ball was now in the court of the classis to nominate a professor for a cause to which it had never been fully committed.

The General Body met in New York on April 25, 1775, to receive the joint recommendation of the Classis of Amsterdam and the theological faculty of Utrecht for an American professor of theology. To no one's surprise, the name suggested was that of John Henry Livingston, minister of the Church in New York. Because of the importance of the question, action was deferred until an October meeting, before which all of the congregations were to be solicited as to their opinion.

Just one week before the April meeting in New York, the "shot heard round the world" had been fired by the embattled farmers at Concord Bridge. It was a skeleton delegation that assembled in New York in October. When the question of the professorship came up, the following action was taken.

By reason of the pitiful condition of our land, the consideration of the subject of the Professorate is deferred.[10]

New Brunswick Seminary might well have been founded in October of 1775, but the struggle for American independence intervened and nine years were to go by before the Reformed Church felt able to examine the question again.

II

The Years in New York

The Treaty of Paris, which recognized the independence of the thirteen colonies from Great Britain, was signed in the early fall of 1783. As soon as possible after that, the general meeting of ministers and elders took up the question of the professorate which the national crisis had forced it to abandon in 1775. At the session in New York in May of 1784 the brethren considered a letter from Queen's College, reminding them of their earlier commitment to that institution. (Those reading the record may be confused by the fact that in the language of the day the college is sometimes referred to as the "Seminary at New Brunswick.") There was also a letter from those intending to begin a college in Schenectady, New York, implying that this new school could well be an appropriate site for the theological professorate.

Faced with three possibilities—an independent professorate, one located in New Brunswick, or one in Schenectady—the general meeting decided to postpone the issue until the following October. In the meantime the subject was to be discussed in every Particular Body, and every minister and elder delegate was to come to a special session to be held in New York on October 5, "in order that then with the Lord's blessing, this weighty matter may be brought to a desirable issue."[1]

Nineteen persons were present for the October meeting, representing the five Particular Bodies of New York, Hackensack, Kingston, New Brunswick, and Albany. After having reviewed all of the previous actions as well as the correspondence received in May, the General Body appointed a committee of six persons to bring in recommendations. That committee, the chairman of which was Jacob Rutsen Hardenbergh, sought to steer a smooth course between the Scylla of New Brunswick and the Charybdis of Schenectady. The recommendation was that Queen's College remain in New Brunswick and that every possible financial assistance be given to the college's trustees. It was further recommended that another committee be appointed to work with the Schenectady consistory in "promoting and carrying into effect" what was to become Union College.

The refusal to associate the theological professorate with either New Brunswick or Schenectady meant that the General Body was reverting to the original proposal of the Classis of Amsterdam for a professorate independent of any school. Since the only congregation which could possibly afford to spare a minister for even part-time service in that capacity was that of New York, the committee recommended that the professor of theology be located in that city. It was very honest in stating its reasons for coming to such a conclusion.

> Since, through the unfavorable nature of the times, the Rev. Body is not in condition to call a Professor upon a sufficient income, it is hoped that the Rev. Consistory of New York will make the best arrangement in relation to it.[2]

The General Body, having drawn the conditions thus closely, then unanimously recommended the appointment of Dr. John Henry Livingston, one of the ministers of the Church in New York, as professor of sacred theology. In view of both the recommendation of the Classis of Amsterdam and the frank admission of the committee that the denomination had no money, that could have come as no surprise. Every student desiring ordination in the Dutch Reformed Church had to study with Dr. Livingston and was required to earn a certificate which entitled him to the preparatory examination (the ancestor of our present "professorial certificate"). Each student receiving the certificate was to give the professor an honorarium of at least five pounds.

Obviously, some arrangement had to be made with the New York church to permit one of its ministers this part-time activity.

A committee was therefore appointed to meet with the consistory of that church for the purpose of

> . . . informing them of the Professoral call made upon their highly esteemed pastor and requesting them to make every possible arrangement to afford him opportunity according to the demands of duty in that position, to accomplish the advancement of the welfare of our beloved Church.

The final recommendation of the committee was that Dr. Hermanus Meyer, minister at Pompton Plains and Totowa, be appointed instructor in the inspired languages.[3] Nothing is said about his honorarium or of any arrangements with his consistory.

It is difficult to say just when the plan approved by the General Body in October of 1784 began to be implemented. Probably nothing happened before Dr. Livingston's formal inauguration, which took place on May 19, 1785, in the Old Dutch Church in Garden Street (now Exchange Place) in New York. His inaugural address, delivered in Latin, was said to be "a learned and elegant dissertation." One may assume that it was only after the inauguration that the new professor began to give instruction in his own home, then located at 79 Broadway.

The first person to complete the course and receive a certificate from Dr. Livingston was John Martin van Harlingen, a 1783 Queen's graduate. He was licensed by the Reverend Christian Synod, which met in New York in October of 1786, and was ordained by the same body the following May, having received a call to the New Jersey congregations of Millstone and Six Mile Run. The meeting of October, 1787, accepted the certificates of five more students, indicating that the new professorate had begun to work satisfactorily.

Before continuing the story further, it might be well to pause for a moment to consider Dr. Livingston's personality and his general theological stance. At the time of his appointment to the professorate in 1784 he was forty-two years old, probably in the

John Henry Livingston

prime of his powers. One of his contemporaries described him this way:

> He must have been dignified as a child, as a boy, as a young man, as well as in his maturer years. . . . His expression of countenance was serene, benevolent, with a slight dash of the aristocratic about it—a dash not assumed, but natural and not disagreeable, for every one that knew him seemed to admit that he at least had a right to it.[4]

This tall aristocratic person, whose very presence apparently attracted and held attention, had been trained first at Yale, from which he graduated in 1762, and then at the University of Utrecht, from which he received the doctorate in sacred theology in 1769. The theological position of Utrecht at that time has been described as one of "rational supernaturalism," a position which accepted all of the canons of orthodoxy but believed they were capable of logical arrangement and defense. It is obvious that in his theological thinking and instruction Dr. Livingston shared the Utrecht point of view. Gabriel Ludlow, one of his last students, has described him in this way:

> The whole of it (theology) was mapped out in its various compartments and the relation of every part was shown to every other part distinctly. Thus every part threw light upon every other part—a light which could not have been thrown upon any part if viewed and treated separately from any other. And if to this you add that a full, clear, precise definition was given to every doctrine and fact embraced in the system and that the student was required to make himself at home upon all this, any thinking, unprejudiced man can appreciate the advantages attending such a course in instruction and the high ability of the man who carried it into effect. The pupils of Dr. Livingston were not required merely to furnish their memories with theological truth, but to exercise their judgments and reasoning powers upon what they had gathered from their wise, good and faithful instructor.[5]

But it must not be assumed that his adherence to the theology of "rational supernaturalism" meant that Dr. Livingston's theol-

ogy was dry and mechanical. There were two other factors which
have to be considered. The year before he left for the Netherlands he had spent in New York, where he came greatly under
the influence of Dr. Archibald Laidlie, the Scotsman who was
minister of the first English-speaking congregation of the Reformed Church. Dr. Laidlie was much involved with evangelical
pietism and repeatedly warned against a theology that had no
effect on the heart.

Also, for the first twenty-six years of his professorate, Dr. Livingston was primarily a pastor. There is absolutely no evidence
that his ministry in New York was considered academically dull.
On the contrary, he was one of the most popular preachers in
the city, one of the reasons why his consistory was loathe to part
with him.

A word must also be said about Livingston's partner in theological instruction, Dr. Hermanus Meyer, who is rather the forgotten man in the professorial operation. German by birth, Meyer
was educated in Groningen and came to serve the church in
Kingston, New York, in 1763. An adherent of the coetus, he ran
afoul of the conferentie majority in his consistory and was forced
out in 1766. After a few years attempting to form a coetus congregation in Kingston, in 1772 he accepted the call to the congregations of Pompton Plains and Totowa in New Jersey. He was
an extremely accomplished linguist whose life-time project was
a new translation of the Old Testament. In 1789 Queen's College
awarded him the honorary degree of doctor of divinity.

Such was the impressive team with which the Reformed Church
began its program of theological education in the New World.
Both Meyer and Livingston were products of the European system of theological training. Both enjoyed reputations in their field
that extended beyond their own immediate circles. The entire
program should have enjoyed smooth sailing from its inception.
It did not and, indeed, at one point it almost foundered. To be
sure, it was following a new and uncharted course, but the sad
fact is that in these early days it never enjoyed the full support
of the Reformed Church.

The first problem was a minor one, almost built into the system which had been designed in 1784. In the original design, a young man studied theology in New York with Dr. Livingston, and the sacred languages in Pompton Plains with Dr. Meyer. Not only did this mean a good deal of commuting in a day in which traveling was not easy, but the cost of living in New York was considerably higher than in Pompton Plains or elsewhere in the country. A number of students therefore had asked the Reverend Christian Synod for permission to study with a minister nearer their home. The question came before the synod at its meeting in New York in October of 1786.

In response, the synod held the line: "Not every minister is sufficiently furnished to impart instruction in these high mysteries besides, the benefit to be expected from a theological college is lost by the students being thus scattered."[6] Synod did, however, make one concession to the petitioners. It appointed Dr. Meyer "lector of most holy theology" and directed that students might study for their certificates either with Dr. Livingston in the city *or* with Dr. Meyer in the country.

At its meeting in New York in October of 1788 the synod further tightened its regulations by passing a rule that no students could be admitted to the theological course unless they previously had earned the bachelor of arts degree. Students lacking that degree would have to submit to an examination and be recommended by their classes before entering the theological program. Such action insured that in the future the overwhelming majority of theological students would be college graduates.

The next crisis was precipitated by the death of Dr. Meyer in October of 1791. Obviously some replacement had to be found or the entire burden would fall on Dr. Livingston in the expensive environment of New York City. Meeting in New York in October of 1792, synod confessed that it had not yet found a way to finance its professorship but acknowledged that in the meantime some provision had to be made for "some of the students of divinity (who) find it exceedingly difficult, on account of deficiency of means, to pursue their studies in the commercial emporium of New York." Accordingly, Solomon Froeligh of Hackensack and Schraalenbergh and Dirck Romeyn of Schenectady were appointed lectors in theology, on a temporary basis. Three very different centers in the church—New York, Schenectady, and Hackensack—were thus available for theological instruction.[7]

In the meantime, the trustees of Queen's College had been reminding synod of its old commitments, asking, rather plaintively, when it would be possible for Queen's to call a professor of theology who would also be the college president, and threatening to unite with Princeton if action were not taken. The synod of 1794 replied that if Queen's were at all serious about having the theological professorate, it would have to move to a place such as Bergen (now Jersey City) where it would be more accessible to a larger part of the Reformed Church. It even appointed a committee to meet with the trustees to work out such a change.

Obviously, the synod did not take this suggestion too seriously because in the same session it worked out a plan to move the theological professorate to the Long Island village of Flatbush where there was already a flourishing academy (Erasmus Hall). Flatbush also had the advantages of a village situated near a city, the "cheapness and retirement peculiar to a village," and "free and easy intercourse with the literary and public characters which abound in a city." All that had to be done was to prevail on the New York consistory to allow Dr. Livingston to preach only once on a Sunday and to give up such pastoral work as would enable him to devote four days a week to serving as professor of theology.[8]

Actually, the arrangement was not quite so novel as it sounded. Dr. Livingston had a summer home in Flatbush and had already been teaching there in the summer and in New York in the winter. The consistory released its minister for half-time service as professor, while he released them from half his salary. In the spring of 1796 the professor moved to Flatbush and began holding his classes there. Everything looked promising, with a student enrollment which rose from seven to fourteen.

Then in 1797 something inexplicable happened. A few words

by way of introduction are necessary first. After its meeting in
June of 1794, the meeting at which the removal of the theological
professor to Flatbush was authorized, the General Synod decided
to meet only once every three years. In the intervening years a
somewhat smaller body met, calling itself the "Particular Synod
of Dutch Reformed Churches in America." It was to this body at
its meeting in New York in October of 1796 that the professor of
theology wrote a letter in which he poured out his heart. His
sense of *noblesse oblige* had failed him. He was weary of being
shunted around from place to place at synodical whim. He was
discouraged by the apparent lack of seriousness about theological
education and did not hesitate to say so.

Dr. Livingston's letter is much too long to be included here,
but the quotation of a few sentences may suffice to indicate its
general tenor.

That I am not at all anxious on my own account is sufficiently
evinced by the silence and passive waiting which has marked my
whole conduct since my appointment to the office; but I confess I am
anxious to see an institution established of whose importance I am so
fully convinced and of whose future existence I now begin to doubt.
I am very anxious for the reputation and honor of our churches who
cannot in justice to their numbers, wealth and character suffer the
whole burden of preparing their candidates to rest upon one individual member. It is not only an ungenerous but a precarious source of
dependence.

Upon the whole, after a candid and partial view of existing facts
and of all that has passed upon the subject, I am constrained to make
the following conclusions:

1. That whatever may have been the serious resolution of those of
1771 who formed the union or of those of 1784 who established the
Professorate . . . , it does not appear to be the intention of our
churches to carry the institution into effect.

2. That as long as I continue with my private exertions to supply
the wants of the public, no measures will be executed for bringing
the Professorate to a due establishment.

3. That if such measures are suffered to slumber much longer, the whole institution will sink into oblivion . . .

The letter concluded with a slightly veiled threat on Livingston's part to suspend all of his classes until the synod made up its mind as to the future.[9]

The particular synod was horrified; it set up machinery to raise money and implored the professor to continue his labors in spite of his discouragement. Truth to tell, this was about the fourth or fifth time that the synod had set up the machinery to raise funds for the professorate and nothing had happened. Small wonder that the good Dr. Livingston had begun to wonder whether the game was worth the candle!

Dr. Livingston's letter and the reaction of the particular synod came to the attention of General Synod at its meeting in New York in June of 1797. The question was frankly raised, "Is it expedient under present circumstances to take any further measures for the support of the Professorate?" The vote was in the negative, whereupon the following recommendations were adopted:

1. That Professor Livingston ought to be immediately informed of the determination of Synod that it is not expedient under present circumstances to take any further measures for the support of the professorate.
2. . . . In consequence of the serious inconveniences which arise from the certificate of a professor being absolutely required for the admission of students to examination, the Synod nominate and appoint two additional Professors of Theology.

To no one's surprise the two lectors, Solomon Froeligh and Dirck Romeyn, were chosen to the office. Now the Reformed Church, far from having a theological college, had three minister-instructors of equal status in three parts of the denomination.[10] Insult was added to injury by the particular synod in 1799 when it appointed John Bassett of Albany and Gerardus Kuypers of New York as teachers of Hebrew.

Dr. Livingston left Flatbush and returned to his home in New York, resuming full pastoral responsibilities with the church there, although continuing to offer instruction to any interested students. A lesser man would have given up the entire operation, leaving the Reformed Church program of ministerial training to fend for itself as best it could. But having put his hand to the plow, he saw no way to turn back even though the way forward seemed uncertain indeed. Some have tried to excuse the actions of the synod of 1797 on the basis of an uncertain economy because of the strained situation with England and France, but the blunt truth is that the Reformed Church was not yet ready to foot the bill for a genuine program of theological education.

A census taken by the General Synod of 1800 revealed that Dr. Romeyn had three students under his tuition, while Domine Froeligh had five; Dr. Livingston reported that he had only one. Once more the synod attempted to raise funds to render the professorate independent. Each member of the denomination was asked to contribute two shillings annually for the next six years, and collectors, who were to retain five percent of whatever they were able to raise, were appointed in every congregation. A pastoral letter outlining the plan and asking for cooperation was sent to every congregation.

Once again, nothing seems to have happened. Part of the reason for this lack of activity seems to have been that circumstances conspired to prevent any meeting of the General Synod in 1803. When the delegates met in Poughkeepsie on June 7, there were such irregularities in the delegation from the Particular Synod of Albany (the present organizational structure of the denomination had been adopted only in 1800) that it was decided to adjourn the meeting and try again the next October in Greenwich Village. But by October a frightening epidemic was raging on Manhattan Island, so the meeting was again postponed until the following May. Even then there was difficulty in getting started. No quorum was present on May 8, 9, or 10. Finally, on May 11, it was decided to send a letter to Mr. Amerman, a delegate from Harlingen, New Jersey, who had not shown up, and request him to attend. By Monday morning, May 14, Mr. Amerman had arrived—and the meeting finally was under way!

Realizing that the actions of the synod of 1797 had been hasty and ill-advised, this synod did its best to correct them. Two additional professors of theology had been chosen by that synod, Froeligh and Romeyn, and that decision could hardly be reversed without many hurt feelings. The synod of 1804, however, pointed out that these had been only temporary expedients to meet an emergency and should either man choose to vacate his office, no successor would be appointed. The synod wished to return to the plan of only one professor of theology. (Dirck Romeyn had died a month earlier, but the synod seemed unaware of that fact.)

Probably to reassure Dr. Livingston of his position, the synod moved to nominate and elect a *permanent* professor of theology who would be located in New York, which the committee was convinced was the only appropriate location at this time. "The objection arising from the expense to students," said the committee, "is more specious than solid." In addition to Dr. Livingston, Dr. Linn, his colleague in the New York ministry, and Solomon Froeligh, Jeremiah Romeyn, and John Bassett were nominated. Needless to say, Dr. Livingston was overwhelmingly elected. It is said that Froeligh's disappointment began the bitterness which ultimately led to his secession from the Reformed Church.[11]

This synod was challenged by a letter from the consistory of the Church in New York, pointing out that the charter of 1754, which was still in force, gave that consistory the power of appointing a professor of theology in Columbia (formerly King's) College. The consistory implied that it was seriously considering exercising this right, though not without synod's approval, since it would afford the professor "support, honor and permanency" and put the establishment on a much more desirable foundation.

One can only speculate as to the reasons why the New York consistory sent this letter. Was it simply a threat made in the hope that it would persuade synod at last to do something? Was it an attempt to unload Dr. Livingston gently? Or was it an effort to protect him from the growing number of candidates for his job? Each of these explanations has some logic, but the true one will never be known. Synod's answer was that

> . . . (they) cannot enter into the proposed plan as they wish not to blend their theological professorate with any other establishment not derived from the immediate authority of the Low Dutch Reformed churches.[12]

Synod did, however, accept the offer of the New York consistory to act as a depository for any funds raised for the support of the professorate.

One small piece of business remained to be done. The old particular synod of 1799 had appointed two teachers of Hebrew, John Bassett and Gerardus Kuypers. Such appointments, however, were the business of General Synod; the appointment of Bassett was continued by this synod, but Kuypers was replaced by Jeremiah Romeyn. Each Hebrew instructor was to receive the sum of five dollars for issuing a certificate of competency to a student.

Perhaps the actions taken may have helped soothe some of Dr. Livingston's wounded feelings, but actually they resulted in very little. In 1806 the committee recommended the appointment of a professor for the Albany area, but after its bitter experiences of the past few years the synod refused to touch the suggestion. The synod of 1806 also went through the same futile gestures of raising funds, but they were really so much empty beating of the air. The same synod received glowing accounts of prospects for church extension in Canada if only the necessary funds could be found. This was a much more attractive possibility than a part-time professor whose generous salary was already being paid by the wealthy church of New York!

The year 1806 seems to have marked the lowest ebb in the fortunes of the theological professorate. In summarizing the mood of the Reformed Church at the time Edward Tanjore Corwin has written

> . . . every expedient seemed to be unavailing. The resolutions and plans of the Synod seemed to be futile. The uncertainty of location

seemed to destroy every effort. The prospects grew faint and dubious. The most sanguine friends of the professorate were ready to despair concerning it.[13]

It was just at this unhappy time, however, that what was the desperation of Queen's College turned out to be the great opportunity for the theological professorate. After a rather fitful existence since its chartering in 1770, the college had suspended operations in 1795. The class of 1794 had numbered five; the class of 1795 had declined to two. Richard McCormick, the Rutgers historian, puts it this way:

After twenty-four years of tenuous existence, the College had expired. Born out of the controversy that had rent the Dutch Church, distracted almost at the outset by the impact of the Revolution, deprived of a president through all but four years of its existence, and frustrated in its efforts to secure consistent denominational support, the wonder is not that the College collapsed but rather that it survived as long as it did.[14]

To be sure, Queen's continued as a paper corporation, but the trustees met only occasionally for routine financial business. Exactly what led to the movement to revive the college is not clear, but the trustees were called into session on March 25, 1807, to consider reopening the institution. The moving spirit seems to have been Andrew Kirkpatrick, the chief justice of New Jersey, but much of the solid work was done by the Rev. Dr. Ira Condict, a Princeton graduate and Presbyterian minister who became domine of the First Church in New Brunswick in 1794.

At this 1807 meeting which decided to reopen the college, it was also voted to raise $12,000 to relocate it in a new building on a new site. To achieve this purpose, agents were sent to the Particular Synods of Albany and New York, whose delegates, aware of the efforts being made on behalf of the professorate and not wanting to see them frustrated by another fund-raising drive, responded to the trustees' appeal with a counterproposal.

. . . that all the moneys subscribed to them (the Trustees) in the State
of New York be a fund exclusively appropriated to the education of
young men for the ministry and the establishment of a theological
school upon such conditions under such stipulations as shall be proposed by the General Synod . . .[15]

The trustees saw little or no alternative to the proposal of the
Particular Synod of New York, especially since most of the wealth
of the denomination was located within the bounds of that body.
Once their consent was obtained, a special meeting of the General Synod was called for September 1, 1807, to meet in the
Church in Harlem. There was the usual difficulty in securing a
quorum so the session did not begin until September 9 when two
brethren from the Particular Synod of Albany arrived to make up
the necessary number. One assumes that the delay was not so
much the result of reluctance to take up the subject as it was of
difficulties of transportation.

After a committee was appointed to consider the proposal, the
synod adjourned to meet the next morning in the consistory room
of the Dutch Church in Garden Street in New York. That meeting, held at 10:00 a.m. on September 10, 1807, was surely one
of the most significant meetings of the General Synod ever held,
since it produced the celebrated "Covenant" which was strongly
to influence the life of the Reformed Church for the next fifty
years.

The full text of the Covenant is too long to reprint here, but
its seven points may be summarized as follows. All moneys raised
in the State of New York were to be devoted to the support of a
theological professorship at Queen's and to scholarships for students for the ministry of the Dutch Church. (Apparently moneys
for the support of Queen's College itself were to be raised in
New Jersey.) Whatever moneys the synod had collected for the
professorate were to be turned over to the Queen's trustees for
that purpose, since it was the intention of the synod to establish
the professorate in New Brunswick as soon as funds were available for his support. A group to be known as "Superintendents

of the Theological Institution in Queen's College" was to be appointed by synod to oversee that aspect of the work and their authority was to be recognized by the trustees. Finally

> The Synod agrees to provide money for a theological library and for the purpose of erecting a theological hall; or to contribute their proportion to the erecting such building or buildings as may be designed for the joint accomodation of the literary and theological departments of the college, providing the sum do not amount to more than would be necessary for erecting a separate building for Professoral Hall.[16]

Knowing the synod's reputation for fund raising, the Queen's trustees may well have kept their fingers crossed! The New York church, however, committed itself to $10,000, and the village congregation in Harlem assumed responsibility for $400. It was a time of hope and excitement for just about everyone in the Reformed Church.

All that remained to be done was to appoint the superintendents, which was done by a ballot election. Those chosen were as follows: *John N. Abeel*, a Princeton graduate and a theological student of both Livingston's and Witherspoon's, now one of the ministers of the New York church; *James V. C. Romeyn*, a graduate of the Schenectady Academy (now Union College) and a theological student of his uncle, Dirck Romeyn, now minister of what had been the conferentie congregation in Schraalenbergh, New Jersey (this must have been another bitter blow to Froeligh); *Jeremiah Romeyn*, who had also studied theology with his Uncle Dirck as well as Dr. Meyer, the domine of Harlem who was also one of the synodical professors of Hebrew; *Thomas G. Smith*, a Scotsman who had been trained in the Associate Reformed Church and was now minister in Bloomingdale and Hurley, New York; *Peter Labagh*, a theological student of both Froeligh and Livingston, now ministering in Catskill; and *John M. Bradford*, a Brown graduate and former Presbyterian, now one of the ministers in Albany. Queen's College was represented by *Dr. Con-*

dict, John S. Vredenburgh, minister at Raritan and a Queen's graduate, as well as a former Livingston student, and *John Schureman,* also a Queen's graduate and a Livingston product, minister in Millstone, New Jersey. To this varied group of nine ministers the future of theological education in the Reformed Church was entrusted.

The committee sent a long letter to all of the churches, rehearsing the whole history of theological education in the Reformed Church as well as the details of the new Covenant.

That letter concluded with the following exhortation.

The plan now submitted forms her [the Reformed Church's] last hope, and the committee are happy in having it in their power to state that this hope has been greatly encouraged by the generous contributions of one portion of her members; its consummation rests with those to whom the application is yet to be made . . . if they value their own souls, if they sympathize with the suffering churches, if they seek the best interest of their children; and above all, if they regard the authority of their Lord, let them combine their prayers and their efforts to support an institution which cannot fail to give extent and stability to the Reformed Church.[17]

III
Partner in the Covenant

In spite of the adoption of the Covenant in 1807, Dr. Livingston showed himself in no hurry to move to New Brunswick. He continued to offer theological instruction in his home in New York. In fact, between 1808 and 1810 he had six students, including one of his own relatives, though he shared several with some of his synodically-appointed colleagues. The question was whether the Queen's trustees and the synod could raise sufficient capital to produce the income for a professor's salary. The $10,000 pledge of the New York consistory had been generous, but that was only a beginning. How would the rest of the church respond?

The Queen's College trustees had not been sitting by idly. In the fall of 1807 they had received the gift of the heirs of James Parker for a five-acre site along Somerset Street in New Brunswick, the present old campus of Rutgers. Having chosen their site, they accepted plans for a building designed by John McComb, a well-known New York architect, and laid the cornerstone on April 27, 1809. The building which was not completed until 1811 is essentially what today is known as "Old Queens." It was designed for the academic work of the preparatory school, the college, and the theological institute. These were located in the central section of the building, while four faculty apartments were located in the two wings.

In August of 1808 the trustees invited Dr. Livingston to be both president and professor of theology, offering him a total salary of $1,000 per annum, $750 as professor and $250 for his duties as president. Since his salary as a New York minister was $2,500 he did not feel that he could take that much of a cut in income and therefore declined the offer. After a short but unsuccessful search for someone else to act as president, an office for which Dr. Livingston had no great enthusiasm, the trustees

33

Old Queens

made a new offer in February of 1810. Because their income-producing capital had increased somewhat, this time the trustees were able to offer a salary of $1,400 for the theological professorate. The salary for the presidency was slightly reduced to $200.

That reduction doubtless reflected the fact that Dr. Livingston had indicated to the trustees that he was willing to undertake only the most minimal responsibilities for administering the college. He was willing to "preside at commencement and authenticate diplomatic documents and take general superintendence of the institution as far as his time and health would admit." Ira Condict, who had already been named vice president, was to carry the real burden of administration. With the exceptions as to his presidential duties understood by the trustees, Dr. Livingston indicated his willingness to move to New Brunswick in the fall of 1810.

For a man of sixty-four to give up the comfort of his New York home and salary and come to what was only a small village for a much smaller income (in December the trustees raised the professorial salary to $1,700 and added a housing allowance of $300) indicated Dr. Livingston's dedication to the cause with which he had been marginally involved for the past twenty-six years. He made few concessions to the times—though fashions were changing rapidly, he continued to wear the knee breeches, silver-buckled shoes, and powdered wig of an eighteenth-century man. He also always carried a cane, though from the sprightliness of his step, he seemed to have little need of it.

In the summer of 1810 Dr. Livingston purchased a home at 59 Albany Street in New Brunswick and began academic work there in October. Five students were enrolled, a number which the following year increased to nine. Academic work was transferred to Old Queens at the beginning of the fall term of 1811. It seemed as though the creation of a "theological institute" in Queen's College had been the right move. Just before he left New York in 1810, Dr. Livingston had written to his old friend Elias Van Bunschooten, the eccentric domine of Sussex County, New Jersey, suggesting that he make a donation to the cause of theological education. Livingston and Van Bunschooten had both been Dutchess County boys and everyone in the area knew about the Van Bunschooten farm and the money which it had yielded.

Several personal interviews followed and in 1814 all of these efforts bore fruit. Domine Van Bunschooten presented the synod with the sum of $14,640, to be kept by the Queen's trustees (the synod was not yet an incorporated body). The interest from the money was designated for assistance to indigent young men preparing for the ministry. That gift, increased to $17,000 at Van Bunschooten's death a year later, gave the theological institute a splendid scholarship fund, even though at many other points it was a financially faltering enterprise.

Professor Livingston's first report to the General Synod was made at its meeting in Albany in June of 1812. He reported that he currently had nine students under his instruction at New Brunswick. Unhappily, two of the nine students did not have the financial resources to continue their studies and therefore had withdrawn to become school teachers. Another student had be-

gun his studies the previous month. He had opened a school in
New Brunswick to support himself and hoped that he would be
able both to attend the theological lectures and teach school. If
all of this has a startlingly modern sound, it must be remembered
that the country had just begun to emerge from a deep depression
which had resulted from President Jefferson's embargo.

Another subject, also concerning finances, was brought up for
discussion at the 1812 synod meeting.

> He [Dr. Livingston] wished to be excused from entering into any
> detail respecting the funds and intended wholly to omit that subject,
> the mention of which, it can readily be conceived, is unpleasant to
> himself and must be distressing to the General Synod; but faithfulness
> to the churches and his duty to inform the General Synod of the facts
> which affect the vital interest of the institution forbid his silence.[1]

The unhappy truth was that of the $4,000 which had been prom-
ised him for the past two years the professor had received about
$1,200. In reporting the situation, however, Livingston made it
clear that he was in no way laying any claim to this unpaid salary.
He was simply trying to state the case, pointing out that in addition to the deficiency in his own salary, there was no money
for scholarships (the Van Bunschooten gift had not yet been made)
or for the purchase of a library.

Once again the synod promised to try to crank up the financial
machinery, though one wonders how seriously that action was
taken after so many empty promises. It did, however, adopt a
"Plan of the Theological School of the Reformed Dutch Church,
established at New Brunswick in New Jersey in connection with
Queen's College." Evidently the committee, headed by James
V. C. Romeyn, had given the matter serious study, for the proposed plan, consisting of five articles, was the basis for the organization of the school for many years.

The first article spelled out the final authority of General Synod
over every aspect of the school. This authority was to be exercised
by a Board of Superintendents consisting of nine persons—three

from the Synod of New York, three from the Synod of Albany, and three from the trustees of Queen's College. The members were to be chosen by ballot every three years. The second article explained the responsibilities of the superintendents, including an annual meeting in New Brunswick at the time of the Queen's College commencement.

Article III clearly stated that the school could not be considered fully organized without a faculty of three. Each faculty member was expected to give three lectures a week and to give six months notice in the event of his resignation. The fourth article laid down certain requirements for students, viz., that they must be members of some Protestant church, that they must be college graduates or pass an academic entrance examination, and that they must submit a paper or a sermon to the professors weekly in rotation.

The final article stated that three years were to be considered the normal course of study and that the academic schedule was to correspond as far as possible with that of Queen's College. The subjects to be covered in that period of time were to include all branches of theology, biblical criticism, church history, church polity, pastoral and practical theology, and fluency in the original languages. At the end of the three years, the students were to be examined by the faculty and superintendents for a professorial certificate or for a longer stay in the school. [2]

It is interesting to compare this curriculum with that of Andover Seminary which had been started by the orthodox Congregationalists in Massachusetts a few years earlier in 1808, or with that of Princeton Seminary which the Presbyterians began in 1812. It is somewhat difficult to make a direct comparison between the New Brunswick curriculum and that of Andover, since Andover was organized on quite a different plan. Each year the students concentrated in a different branch of theological learning. The first year was given over to biblical studies, including Hebrew, the second year to the various topics of theology, and the final year to church history and homiletics. Two professors shared the teaching responsibilities.

Princeton's curriculum was organized a year at a time after its inception in 1812. At the beginning there was only one professor, who taught Hebrew and English Bible. Other faculty and subjects were added as new students were enrolled. The first catalogue, which appeared in 1812, indicated that the faculty now numbered three: one member was in charge of theology, one of church history and polity, and the third was in charge of the original languages. As in the case of New Brunswick, each student was to submit a composition or sermon weekly.

While nothing more than a general comparison can be made, it is clear that the curriculum requirements outlined by the superintendents at New Brunswick in 1812 bear comparison with those of Andover and Princeton. The only problem was that until 1815 the faculty, with the exception of the year 1812-3, was composed of only one person.

One final piece of business remained for the committee. Ever since 1804 instruction in Hebrew had been offered by Dr. John Bassett, apparently a competent scholar. Bassett, however, had been appointed under the old system and his church was at Boght near Albany. One wonders how many students came to him after the professorate moved to New Brunswick. Apparently Dr. Bassett realized the problem for he offered his resignation to the synod in 1812. With the new location in New Brunswick, it had become important to find a Hebrew instructor somewhere in the area.

It must have gratified Dr. Livingston that the choice fell upon John M. van Harlingen, who was living in Millstone where he had been minister. It will be remembered that van Harlingen was Livingston's first graduate in 1786. The synod elected him professor of Hebrew and church history; he accepted the Hebrew chair and agreed to a temporary assignment in church history. Since he had no other responsibilities he was able to devote full time to his academic duties. A contemporary says that he had a sufficient patrimony to make "all attention to pecuniary gain unnecessary." Though van Harlingen was virtually a second faculty member, he received no stipend except for the fees which were paid him by the students. What had seemed to be an almost ideal arrangement was, however, rudely terminated in June of 1813 by van Harlingen's sudden and unexpected death.

In the meantime things had not been going well at the college. The death of Dr. Condict, the vice president, in June of 1811 seems to have dealt it almost a mortal blow since he had been the enthusiastic administrator of the college while Dr. Livingston's position was largely honorific. Dr. John Schureman, one of the ministers of the Church in New York, was almost immediately called to be Condict's successor. A graduate of Queen's in the class of 1795 and a Livingston student, Schureman came from a family which had supported the college from the beginning. But his health was chronically poor and he simply could not find the physical strength for extensive duties. For a short time he tried to combine his college work with the pastorate of the New Brunswick congregation. He soon realized, however, that this was too taxing and confined himself to the college where in addition to carrying out the vice presidential duties he served as professor of moral philosophy and belles-lettres.

The financial problems of the college soon seemed overwhelming. The cost of the new building, together with the costs of maintaining a college faculty and a theological professor, were simply too much for a student body that never numbered more than thirty. Various proposals for some new form of organization were discussed, but none came to fruition. The only possible solution to the problem was resisted for as long as possible, but it finally had to be faced. Commencement was held in September of 1816, but no further classses were held after that. Once again Queen's College passed out of existence and its building was left to the use of the preparatory school and the theological institute.

The years between 1812 and 1816 had not been totally bad ones for the theological school. In addition to Van Bunschooten's gift another $2,000 was received from Rebecca Knox for purposes of student aid. In 1814 synod appropriated $100 for the purchase of books for the library. The theological library had really begun in 1787 when the synod had appropriated fifteen pounds

. . . for the procuring of some necessary textbooks, here with difficulty obtained, for the use of those gentlemen who are pursuing their
theological studies under the care of the Professor and Lector.[3]

The synod of 1794 had directed Dr. Livingston to serve as librarian for the collection which doubtless he had taken with him
when he moved to New Brunswick.

Before any real progress could be made, an old difficulty once
again had to be faced. The waning of Queen's College meant that
those in the Reformed Church who had never favored the location of the theological school there began agitating for its removal
back to New York. The New York church in particular had never
trusted the way the Queen's trustees spent their money and had
virtually ceased to give to the New Brunswick institutions. Others
felt that the impending failure of the college would leave the
church with an unnecessarily large building to maintain.

For a time Livingston, himself a New Yorker at heart, had
been attracted by the idea, but on more mature reflection he
decided that things had gone too far for another change in location
and all the uncertainty that would accompany it. In a September 1, 1813, letter to Isaac M. Kip, a former parishioner and one
of the leaders of the movement to return the school to New York,
Livingston wrote:

> . . . Nothing positive with respect to the ultimate location ought to
> be immediately adopted. The subject in all its bearings is interesting
> in the highest degree to the peace of the churches and very important
> to myself: but unless I know more of the progress and precise object
> of your friendly consultations or until my advice be requested, it
> would be an improper anticipation to suggest any particular idea of
> sentiment.[4]

The question, however, came up once more when the college
had suspended activity in 1816. The New York church proposed
to the synod of 1817 that it would give $6,000 annually to the
theological school if it would relocate to New York. But the Queen's

trustees, who were holding both the Van Bunschooten and the Knox moneys, as well as other gifts to the professorial fund, stated that this was a violation of the Covenant of 1807, and that they would relase no moneys to support a theological school except in connection with Queen's College. The challenge, together with the fact of recent developments at New Brunswick, put the question of a New York location permanently to rest.

It was the report of the Board of Superintendents to the synod of 1814 that first produced some kind of action.

. . . some very important branches of a theological education cannot be pursued with all desirable advantage on account of a deficiency in the contemplated number of professors. Professor Livingston by his faithfulness and diligence deserves the gratitude of the Church and Synod; but the duties are too extensive and various for one person; and even if he were willing to undertake them, the relief of this aged and venerable teacher, the plan of the School, its respectability and usefulness, together with the reputation and interests of the Church at large require the establishment of at least another Professorship.[5]

The committee went on to report that it had learned from the Queen's College trustees that the consistory of the Church in Albany was willing to give $750 a year for six years and the consistory of the Church in New Brunswick $200 a year for a similar time, for the purpose of a second professorship. With an eye squarely on the Church in New York, the committee asked

Could some of our endowed churches be induced to aid with their substance in this pious design and establish a Professorship which would embrace the Hebrew Language, Biblical Criticism and Ecclesiastical History, the School would present to the Church all reasonable advantages for an adequate education for the gospel ministry . . .[6]

The committee urged the synod to set up a second professorship, an idea which was adopted in principle, waiting to see whether other churches would match the generosity of Albany and New Brunswick. Apparently they did, for at the synod of 1815 Dr.

John Schureman was appointed professor of pastoral theology and ecclesiastical history at a salary of $1,200 and use of an apartment in the college building. Whether Schureman was anxious to be relieved of his strenuous duties at Queen's or whether he saw the end of the college approaching, he readily accepted and was installed in his office in November of 1815. Now for the first time in its thirty-one-year history the school was able to claim a full-time faculty of two for its student body of nineteen.

Once the synod had permanently laid to rest the attempts to relocate the school in New York, as it did in October of 1817, the struggle for stronger financial support could begin in earnest. The same synod which rejected the move to New York also urged that congregations form Cent societies, the contributions of which could be used to make up the deficits in endowment income. A number of such societies were formed and did a fine job for the school's budget, but the real task of raising an adequate endowment still had to be faced.

Before that effort could get under way, the school faced a vacancy in the second professorship by reason of the death of Dr. Schureman on May 15, 1818. He was not quite forty years of age, and had been in poor health for some time. It had been hoped, however, that the removal of all duties except teaching might have helped him to overcome his difficulties. His death meant that temporary help had to be found for Livingston, who was now in his seventy-second year (and had outlived many associates), while a search was made for a successor to Schureman.

After several invitations that proved fruitless, the synod at its session in 1819 chose John Ludlow, pastor of the First Church in New Brunswick, to be professor of biblical literature and ecclesiastical history. A graduate of Union College and New Brunswick, Ludlow was a young man of twenty-six at the time of his appointment. His youth must have been an attractive counterpart of Livingston's age and dignity; in any event there is no indication that the two men did not get along well together.

One of the reasons why there had been so much tension between General Synod and the Queen's trustees was the simple fact that synod was not a corporate body and therefore was unable to hold invested funds or real estate. The suspicion that the trustees who held the funds for the theological school were using them for the expenses of the college was always there and had flared out more than once since the Covenant of 1807. In 1819 the New York legislature granted the synod corporate powers. This corporate status meant that the school was now able to appeal to wealthy New Yorkers who had previously been suspicious of the integrity of the Queen's trustees.

Although he was in his seventy-sixth year, Dr. Livingston began greasing the wheels to get the synod of 1822 to raise an endowment of $25,000 in New Jersey, New York, and Long Island. He was certain that 100 subscriptions of $250 each could be obtained easily in this area, and his pen was busy writing letters to significant ministers and elders to help him persuade the synod to get moving. His principal aim was not only to get the synod to approve the goal of $25,000 but to entrust the responsibility for raising it to competent laymen.

No one can say that the three men appointed were Dr. Livingston's choices, but certainly all three were well known to him and all three were closely related to Queen's. Abraham Van Nest and Isaac Heyer were both New York businessmen, active in the New York church, while Jacob Hardenbergh, the son of the old domine who had been so active in the beginning of Queen's, was a New Brunswick lawyer and president of the Bank of New Brunswick.

These three men and Dr. Livingston went to work with a will and were able to report in 1823 that a total of $26,675 had been subscribed for the endowment. The New York consistory had given $5,000; Dr. Livingston and several others had put themselves down for $500, but the vast majority of subscriptions, as the professor had foreseen, were for $250, many of these from ministers whose salaries were not all that great, averaging $400 or $500 a year.

When one considers the repeated failure of the synod to raise funds in the past, this oversubscription must have produced a great deal of excitement. Of course, the situation was different: times were better economically, the New York question had been laid to rest, and the synod was now able to control its own funds. The important point was that the Reformed Church in New Jersey and New York had at last given solid indication that it was taking theological education seriously. Could the churches in the Synod of Albany, much further away from the scene of the action, be counted upon to respond with similar generosity?

Before that question could be addressed, there was an event at the school which directly affected its relationshp with the Albany area. In the summer of 1822 Professor Ludlow received and accepted a call from the First or North Church of Albany. This call came just at the beginning of the fund-raising drive in which, obviously, the professor did not quite believe since he cited the uncertainty of support as his principal reason for leaving. Doubtless there were also some theological reasons for his leaving, but these did not surface until much later.

Ludlow's resignation, presented to a special meeting of synod held in the fall of 1822, was refused. The synod pointed out to Ludlow that $22,000 of the fund had already been subscribed, with more to come, and stated that they felt it was his duty to remain with the school. He therefore withdrew his resignation and his acceptance of the Albany call. The Albany consistory protested the decision and asked for a reconsideration by the synod of June of 1823, raising the question whether a General Synod had the right to defeat the call of a consistory in this way. Since the synod was about to mount a second drive in the churches of the Synod of Albany and could hardly afford to offend the powerful First Church consistory, it thought better of its earlier decision and released Professor Ludlow to go to Albany.

Since the money for a second professorship was now at hand, the same synod which released Professor Ludlow to the First Church of Albany appointed the Rev. John De Witt, pastor of the Second or South Church of Albany, to be his successor. A Princeton graduate, De Witt had studied theology privately and been ordained in the Congregational Church from which he had

John De Witt

been called to Albany. In his mid-thirties when he came to New Brunswick in 1823, the enthusiastic and animated De Witt soon caught the student fancy. One of his former students described him in this way:

> . . . truly a man of genius and finely cultivated taste as well as capital scholarly attainments. His had not been the advantages of early theological culture, as those now enjoyed, but he made up for all by most assiduous study of the best authors and critics of the day.[7]

It may be inserted parenthetically that Professor De Witt was an enthusiastic gardener and horticulturalist. The oldest shade trees on the Queen's campus were planted by him, and the students always delighted in the flowers in the garden next to his apartment. He also added a subject to the curriculum which was much appreciated by the students—instruction in elocution.

The synod of 1823 gave Professor Ludlow a new job: it made him chairman of the fund-raising drive in the Synod of Albany. Following the example of the New York drive, two prominent laymen made up the rest of the committee—Christian Miller, a prominent Albany businessman, and Abraham Van Dyck, a widely-known and highly-respected lawyer from Coxsackie. Everyone was surprised when the committee reported in 1824 that it had slightly exceeded the results of the New York drive and had raised a total of $26,715, making the possibility of a third professorship a real one.

One more significant event occurred during Dr. Livingston's

tenure. By 1823 the Queen's College trustees reluctantly realized
that they had to take some action before the college building was
sold at auction. There were debts on the edifice which the trustees simply could not pay and the bank was pressing hard. An
agreement was worked out whereby synod assumed responsibility for the mortgage ($4,000 plus interest) and forgave the trustees
an amount of $2,212 which had long been in dispute between
them. A synod committee took charge of the building (legal title
could not pass until 1827 when the New Jersey legislature passed
a special act enabling General Synod, a New York corporation,
to own real estate in New Jersey) and spent some $2,300 redeco-
rating and refinishing all of the rooms except those on the third
floor. To all intents and purposes what is now Old Queens became
the property of General Synod in 1823, though the final title
could not be passed till 1827.

Dr. Livingston must have been ready to sing his *Nunc Di-
mittis*. After years of persistent struggle and much frustration and
disappointment, the school for which he had given his life now

Old Queens Today

had the financial resources to support a faculty of three; the student body now numbered about twenty; for all purposes, after 1823 the theological college had its own building. It was almost as though the old man had refused to die until things he had worked for so laboriously had come into place.

Dr. Livingston lectured to his class on January 19, 1825, and the next morning his grandson found him dead in his bed. He was in his seventy-ninth year, having been born on May 30, 1746. His death literally marked the end of an era not only for the school but for the entire Reformed Church. In addition to the theological school, Dr. Livingston had given the Reformed Church its hymn book, its constitution, and years of quiet stability and strength. The age of the patriarchs was now ended, but at least this Moses had been allowed to enter and enjoy his promised land.

IV

Master of the Covenant

It says much for the stability which Dr. Livingston had brought to the institution that his unexpected death seems in no way to have interrupted the work at New Brunswick. For the remainder of the academic term in 1825 a large burden fell on Professor De Witt who, in addition to his own subjects, took full responsibility for instruction in didactic and polemic theology. In the summer of that year he also took full responsibility for examining and certifying the four students who had completed their studies and were ready for examinations by their classes.

One of Dr. De Witt's chief assets was his enthusiastic love of books. His own personal library, which was purchased by the school from his widow after his death in 1831, provided the first nucleus of a good theological collection. As early as 1821, however, Dr. De Witt had been instrumental in persuading Mrs. Margaret Chinn of Albany to donate 140 volumes to the library in an "elegant mahogany bookcase." (The books are still in the library; the fate of the "elegant bookcase" is unknown!) In a very real sense Dr. De Witt can be called the grandfather of the library which we have today.

Dr. De Witt could be sure that the time of his sole responsibility would be brief because the synod wasted no time in choosing Dr. Livingston's successor. At a meeting on February 17, it appointed Dr. Philip Milledoler, one of the ministers of the Church in New York, as professor of theology, and he assumed his duties at the end of May.

Dr. Milledoler was the son of Swiss immigrants to New York who had been successful in the business world there. Brought up in the German Reformed Church in New York, Dr. Milledoler was a graduate of Columbia (1793) who studied for the ministry

Philip Milledoler

with his pastor and was ordained by the German Reformed Synod
in 1794. From 1795 to 1800 Milledoler had served as pastor of
his home church on Nassau Street in New York, from which he
was called to the Pine Street Presbyterian Church in Philadelphia. The Rutgers Street Presbyterian Church in New York called
in 1805, and the Collegiate Church in New York invited him to
serve there in 1813. The University of Pennsylvania conferred
the honorary doctor of sacred theology degree on Dr. Milledoler
in 1805.

The new professor had had a small brush with theological education earlier when the German Reformed Synod of 1820 had
chosen him to organize its new theological school and to serve as
professor of theology. He ultimately declined but only after he
had kept the synod waiting two years for an answer. Milledoler's
enemies said that he had held out to see if something similar
would develop at New Brunswick, but that could well be a rumor
after the fact.

Just fifty years of age when he left New York, Dr. Milledoler brought all kinds of new energy to his position. One of his first tasks was to provide some decent accommodations for himself and his family in the east wing of Old Queens. After living for some years in Philadelphia and New York in comfortable parsonages, Mrs. Milledoler was so shocked when she saw the decrepit bleakness of her new home that she "burst into a flood of tears."

Far more than material repairs were at stake, however. As early as 1815, Dr. Livingston had proposed a plan for creating at Queen's a "theological college" in which the theological professors would teach part time in the undergraduate department, thus making the college, as Dr. McCormick has said, "an appendage to the theological school." Dr. Livingston's plan never got off the ground, partly because in 1815 the trustees were about to suspend the college.

In 1825, with the arrival of Dr. Milledoler, the plan was revived. In June of that year, a third theological professor was elected in the person of Selah S. Woodhull, minister of the Church in Brooklyn. Thus, for the first time in its history the school could be termed "fully organized," since it had a full-time faculty of three. At a special session held in September of that year, the Covenant of 1807 was rewritten as the Covenant of 1825.

Under the terms of the new Covenant, Dr. Milledoler was elected president of the college, and the synod assumed much larger responsibilities for the operation of the college as well as of the theological institution; in fact, it assumed virtual veto power over the actions of the trustees who were to provide (and pay for) two professors, one of mathematics and one of languages. As part of the enterprise, the three synodical professors of theology were to offer part-time instruction at the undergraduate level. There was to be a committee of six persons—three trustees and three synod appointees—to oversee the entire operation; the undergraduate division, theological institution, and preparatory school were all to share in the facilities of Old Queens, which remained the property of General Synod.

Since the trustees were determined to reopen the college as soon as possible, the supervising committee made the following faculty appointments. In addition to theology, Dr. Milledoler was to teach moral philosophy and evidences of Christianity in the college. Dr. De Witt, professor of biblical literature, was assigned the undergraduate departments of logic, belles-lettres, and elements of criticism, while Professor Woodhull, newly appointed to the theological chair of church history, undertook to teach metaphysics and philosophy as well. The only *quid pro quo* was that the Rev. William Craig Brownlee, a Scotsman from Basking Ridge, New Jersey, the newly-appointed college professor of languages, was to instruct theological students in Hebrew and Greek.

The most lasting result of the Covenant of 1825 was at the time considered least important. For some time everyone had realized that the name "Queen's" was an anomaly for an institution in the American republic, but since the college had led such a shadowy existence no one had bothered to do anything about it. Its 1825 resurrection seemed the right time for activity. Dr. Milledoler was well acquainted with Colonel Henry Rutgers, a prominent Dutch Reformed layman in New York, and something of a philanthropist. On his former minister's urging, Rutgers deposited a bond for $5,000 with the synod, stipulating that the income was to be used for the annual support of the college. He also purchased a bell for the cupola of the college building. Incidentally, the cupola had never been completed, but now in this day of new things, its completion was paid for by Stephen Van Rensselaer, the last patroon of Albany. The cupola and bell still adorn the building which is known today as Old Queens.[1]

There was another unforeseen result of the Covenant of 1825—a matter of nomenclature. Ever since 1784 no one had quite known what to call what had been created. So long as it was an unattached faculty, it was generally called the "theological professorate." Once it became part of Queen's in 1810, the rather cumbersome phrase "theological institution in Queen's College" was often used. After the collapse of the college in 1816, it seemed simpler to refer to the "theological college." But with the revival of the college in 1825 as "Rutgers College," itself by design a "theological college," what was the best way in which to refer to the theological department?

After 1825 the word "seminary" begins to appear in the records as referring directly to the theological school. (It had been used earlier to refer to almost any kind of educational enterprise.) Andover had adopted the term when it was organized in 1808, to be followed by Princeton in 1812. Harvard and Yale, when they came to organize separate departments, chose the name "divinity school." The New Brunswick school evidently felt that it had more in common with Andover and Princeton than with Harvard and Yale. No official action was ever taken, but after 1825 the word seminary was more and more frequently employed to refer to the theological department.

The new creation got under way on November 14, 1825, with thirty students enrolled in the college and nineteen in the seminary. Almost immediately there were some changes in faculty. Mr. Brownlee, the college professor of languages, resigned in 1826 to accept a call to the Collegiate Church in New York where he replaced his president, Dr. Milledoler. Professor Woodhull died on February 27, 1826, three months after he had moved to New Brunswick. Only thirty-nine years old at the time of his death, his sudden and unexpected passing left a large void in the college and seminary alike.

Not wanting to lose any of the momentum which had been

James Spencer Cannon

gained, the synod met in New York on March 29, 1826, and chose as Dr. Woodhull's successor one of the most colorful men ever to be part of its theological faculty, the Rev. James Spencer Cannon, pastor of the Church in Six Mile Run, New Jersey. A native of the island of Curacao, Professor Cannon had never attended college but had studied theology with both Froeligh and Livingston. Dr. McCormick's description of him is worth quoting.

> A gentleman of the old school, largely self-educated, he clung until his death in 1852 to the dress and manners of the Federal era—knee breeches, silk stockings, silver buckles, and a stiff, broad brimmed hat. Dignified but kindly in manner, and a fervent Democrat in politics, he won the affection of the students for his warm interest in their affairs and for his able teaching of metaphysics and the philosophy of the human mind.[2]

At the synod meeting in Philadelphia (where there was now a strong Reformed Church presence) in June of 1827 everything seemed to be moving along well. The Committee on the State of the Churches reported in glowing terms.

> Another subject which calls for gratitude to God and is intimately connected with the state and interests of religion is the prosperous state of our Literary and Theological College. By the generosity of the members and friends of the Church, the subscriptions for the support of the third Professor are in great forwardness. The Literary Department is in full and very prosperous operation and offers the certain prospect of being an abundant fountain whose streams shall supply our Theological Seminary and flowing abroad will gladden many a waste and solitary place of Zion and many a parched and barren spot in the destitute world.[3]

Whatever the committee may have meant by "in great forwardness," the fact was that the moneys raised so enthusiastically for the second and third professorships had largely been in pledges and not in cash. Despite the best efforts of all concerned, payments on pledges were slow in coming in, with the result that

the cost of three theological professors' salaries and the maintenance of the building for which synod had assumed responsibility
were beginning to be worrisome.

The Collegiate Church in New York came to the rescue in 1825
by pledging $1,750 a year, for three years, to the seminary bud-
get, in full expectation that at the end of three years enough
should have been realized from pledges to enable the school to
be self-supporting. That that was not the case is evident from the
synod of June, 1828, which appointed a committee of seven persons "to make application to that Consistory for their continuance
of the same favor for a few years longer."[4] The same synod adopted
an enlarged "Plan for the Theological School." The new plan
contained no basic modifications of that of 1812 but it did include
some new items which are of interest.

Once again the plan authorized a common calendar with Rutgers College and specified the contents for each one of the three
years of instruction.

Year 1: Critica Sacra, Biblical Antiquities, Sacred Geography, Com-
          position, Original Languages, History of the Old Testament,
          Homiletics.
Year 2: Didactic and Polemic Theology, Hermeneutics, Church His-
          tory, Original Languages continued.
Year 3: Didactic and Polemic Theology, Pastoral Theology, Church
          History, Polity, Hermeneutics and Original Languages
          (concluded).

(A catalogue of Princeton Seminary from about the same time
indicates that the two institutions had very nearly the same
curriculum.)

The supplementary material in the 1828 plan also included the
requirement for an annual examination and for "anniversary exercises" in which each graduating senior was to take part—a kind
of protocommencement. The final requirement which was to cause
difficulty in just a few years was that Marck's *Medulla* was to be
used as a textbook in theology.[5]

The synod of 1829 learned that the consistory of the Collegiate churches was willing to continue its extra commitment of $1,750 for an additional year. Since that grant was to expire in the coming November, the synod urged that every member of the denomination be asked to give twenty-five cents a year for the cause of theological education. The Committee on Professorate agreed and recommended the appointment of agents in every classis to secure the funds needed to support the faculty as well as an additional $1,000 for the increase of the library.

The sad fact learned by the synod in 1830 was that all of these drives had yielded the grand total of $734.20, not quite half of the Collegiate Church grant, which was not renewed after 1829. The trustees of the General Synod also asked the church to face up to the fact that approximately $10,000 of the money pledged to the two drives of a decade or so earlier were doubtless uncollectable. The only solution to the problem which they could offer was to assess each congregation twenty-five cents per member for the cause of theological education—a solution which was of course totally unacceptable to the synod. It almost seemed as though things were slipping back to the sad state in which they had been fifteen or twenty years earlier.

Back in September of 1829 the Board of Corporation (the trustees of General Synod) had appointed Mr. William Schuneman to act as its agent to collect funds in classes and congregations in the Hudson Valley. Well satisfied with his success, the board gave him a larger commission the following year and was able to report to the synod in 1831 that Schuneman had been able to collect $1,971 on pledges made in the earlier drives, $2,436 in new pledges, and $1,339 in cash donations, a total of almost $6,000, of which $3,310 was in cash.

The appointment of Schuneman and his apparent success was really the beginning of a series of minor skirmishes between two groups for control of the seminary. On the one hand was the Board of Direction of the Corporation, to give it its full title. This group, composed mostly of laymen (the celebrated Colonel Rutgers was a member until his death), held all of the assets and was responsible for any deficits. The other group, the Committee on Professorate, largely clerical in its composition, was appointed at each synod to represent the superintendents and the faculty. They felt it was their duty to set the seminary program and let the Board of Direction figure out how to pay for it, while the Board of Direction had just the opposite idea; it would set the budget and the other group should trim the program accordingly.

Matters came to a head in the synod of 1831 when the Board of Direction suggested the following.

> The Board are under a deep impression that if General Synod would commit to them the *sole power* of raising funds for the Theological Seminary in such manner as they would think most eligible and would assist their exertions by a strong recommendation to the Churches to cooperate in the measure, a sum sufficient might be raised, in addition to the permanent fund already established, to answer all the necessities of our Theological College. . . . The Board respectfully submit the same to the serious consideration of General Synod.[6]

Faced with that challenge and with Schuneman's success, the Committee on Professorate had no alternative but to agree that the experiment should be tried for a year.

In the midst of this financial skirmishing, however, there was a new crisis occasioned by the unexpected death on October 11, 1831, of Dr. De Witt. Though he had not yet reached the age of forty-two, Dr. De Witt had become a very credible representative of the institution. There can be no doubt that he had inspired the confidence of givers, especially in the Albany area. Probably that was the reason for a strong invitation to Dr. John Ludlow to return to the faculty from his Albany pastorate, an invitation which he had received and declined on a previous occasion. This time he again declined the invitation offered in November of 1831, although he did not make his decision known for several months. The same special session which elected Dr. Ludlow also appointed a special committee to raise the funds necessary to purchase Dr. De Witt's library for the seminary.

Because of Dr. Ludlow's refusal of the offer of a chair in the theological faculty, the synod which met in June of 1832 still faced the problem of finding a successor to Professor De Witt. A number of candidates were placed in nomination but after several ballots, the number was reduced to two. The record does not state the name of the second candidate, but the choice fell on Dr. Alexander McClelland, the professor of languages in Rutgers College. In terms of the Covenant of 1825, Dr. McClelland, while a college professor, had been teaching Hebrew in the seminary where he had been well received. He had also acted as librarian for the joint collection of the two schools and had introduced the first, if somewhat primitive, system of cataloguing. According to McCormick's history,

> Methodically, he (Dr. McClelland) arranged all the volumes into ten classes, each of which occupied a separate portion of the shelves, and with the assistance of a theologue endeavored with moderate success to enforce system and order.[7]

The new professor had not come from a Reformed Church background but was from the Associate Reformed Church, a Presbyterian body with which the Reformed Church was in close relationship. A native of Schenectady and a graduate of Union College, Dr. McClelland had been prepared for the ministry by Dr. John Mason. His first and only pastorate was the Rutgers Street Presbyterian Church in New York, where he succeeded Dr. Milledoler. His old mentor, Dr. Mason, had in the meantime become president of Dickenson College in Carlisle, Pennsylvania, and had invited his former student to join the faculty there in 1822. As a Presbyterian institution, however, Dickenson College did not seem viable, so in 1829 Dr. McClelland had accepted the Rutgers professorship (obviously he and Milledoler must have been well acquainted), from which he was chosen professor of biblical literature and oriental languages in the seminary by the synod of 1832.

Dr. McClelland's election put the first strain on the terms of the Covenant of 1825. At his suggestion, General Synod recommended to the Rutgers trustees that Dr. McClelland be relieved of all duties in the college, which was requested to make other arrangements for filling the vacancy which he was leaving. That action was followed (at an adjourned meeting the following October) by an even more drastic resolution which carried by a vote of twenty-nine to fifteen.

> *Resolved*, that a Committee be appointed to inquire whether the connection existing between the Theological Seminary and Rutgers College be in its present form beneficial to the grand object proposed by the endowment of said Seminary, and to confer on the necessity of a change: and if it be necessary, on the practicability and form of its modification or the expediency of its entire abolition.[8]

In response to this action, synod appointed a committee of five persons. Dr. John Ludlow was the chairman, with Dr. John Knox of New York and the Rev. James Romeyn of Six Mile Run, New Jersey, as the other clerical members. The two elders appointed to the committee were both friendly to Rutgers—Peter Vroom who lived in the area and Abraham Van Nest of New York, who had given so much of his time and money to the welfare of the institutions at New Brunswick. The stage was set for some fireworks at the synod of 1833.

From the point of view of the synod, Rutgers College had been a disappointment. The synod had purchased the building, paid off the college's debts, and lent its theological faculty to be part-time college instructors, all with a view of providing a steady stream of candidates for the seminary. The facts, however, indicated that the entire effort had produced very little. In the eight years between the reopening of the college in 1825 and the report of the Ludlow committee in 1833, a total of forty-four students had graduated from the seminary. The breakdown of their college degrees is as follows: Rutgers, seventeen; no college, nine; Union College, eight. Amherst and Princeton had provided two graduates each; the other graduates came from backgrounds as varied as Columbia, Yale, Dickenson, Belfast, and Glasgow! Toward the end of the period the number of Rutgers alumni had been increasing and the number of Union alumni diminishing, and it was from that trend that the Rutgers trustees made their case.

The Rutgers trustees reported to the synod of 1833, before the Ludlow committee and made the most of their opportunity. They painted the most glowing picture possible of the religious vitality of the college.

> [We] are entirely persuaded that the young gentlemen connected with the College enjoy the best opportunities of literary instruction; and are happy to learn that an efficient Bible Society is in operation— that Biblical recitation and Chapel worship on the Sabbath are punctually attended to—that an association of students for prayer exists; and that a general seriousness pervades the institution. The Synod will hear with gratification that eight young gentlemen, alumni of the College, are now about to enter the Theological School.[9]

The trustees were also able to announce the appointment of Dr. Jacob J. Janeway, a semi-retired Presbyterian minister, as vice president to relieve Milledoler of some of his administrative duties.

The special Ludlow committee had to report that it was hopelessly deadlocked. Ludlow and Romeyn had submitted one report, while Knox and Van Nest had submitted another. (One wonders what happened to Vroom? Knowing that his could be the deciding vote, did he decide to stay away?) The assumption must be that Ludlow and Romeyn had recommended the separation of the seminary from the college, and that Knox and Van Nest had recommended the continuation of the Covenant. Synod's committee gave both groups permission to withdraw their recommendations and then proceeded to make its own.

Perhaps this action was a little unfair since a member of the deadlocked special committee, Dr. Knox of New York, had appeared personally to speak to the report of the Rutgers trustees, a body of which he was a member. In any event, the Synodical

Committee on Professorate (of which Ludlow and Vroom were both members) expressed its joy at the Rutgers report, especially at the fact that Dr. Janeway's appointment would relieve Dr. Milledoler of the "perplexing duties of the government and police of the College," and urged that the Covenant arrangement be retained. Even so, the vote of the synod to accept this report was very close—thirty-two to twenty-eight.

Behind the closeness of the vote was a growing number of people in the Reformed Church who were unhappy with the administration of the college and the theological teaching at the seminary; in a word, they were unhappy with Dr. Milledoler. The leader of this group was Dr. John Ludlow, minister of the First Church in Albany and soon-to-be provost of the University of Pennsylvania. Dr. Ludlow resented the point of view in the Reformed Church called "ultra," a position held not only by the ministers of the Church in New York but by some of the theological faculty as well. "Ultras" were those who accepted and defended the situation as it had been and refused to make any changes. Dr. Ludlow was determined to wrest the control of the seminary from their hands. He lost the battle of 1833, but those who knew his strength and tenacity were sure that he would return to try again.

The General Synod which met in New York in 1834 had before it the first accusation of heresy made against a theological professor in the fifty-year history of the school. Dr. McClelland, the recently chosen professor of biblical literature, had preached a sermon on "Spiritual Renovation Connected with the Use of

Alexander McClelland

Means," which was later published by a New Brunswick printer. The Classis of New Brunswick, while not making any definite accusation, asked the synod to look at the sermon and determine its orthodoxy.

What prompted the Classis of New Brunswick to make such a request is not known. Perhaps it was a genuine concern for the integrity of the faith; perhaps it was a political move intended to get at the theological faculty. In any event, the whole affair came to the Committee on Professorate, the chairman of which was— Dr. John Ludlow!

Dr. McClelland's sermon was typical of the evangelical theology of the time, but that kind of evangelicalism, common as it was in the American church of the day, was difficult to reconcile with the traditional Reformed stance on total depravity and the irresistibility of grace. The professor was asked to make an explanation before the synod which he did in an extensive statement (the printed version occupied seven and one-half pages). On the basis of the sermon and Dr. McClelland's explanatory statement, Dr. Ludlow's committee came up with the surprising recommendation to condemn the sermon but to express confidence in the orthodoxy of the professor on the basis of his explanatory statement!

The committee's recommendation seemed a happy compromise which everyone could accept and thus the first heresy charge in the history of the seminary ended peacefully. The fact was that the synod was about to embark on a concerted effort to raise $30,000 for the seminary which had continued to do such deficit spending that the Board of Direction had had to borrow money to pay its bills. For this great effort a united front was necessary.[10]

Great was the rejoicing, therefore, at the synod of 1835 when the special committee which had been headed by the ever-faithful Abraham Van Nest was able to report that a total of $34,050 had been raised in pledges. To avoid the problem of unpaid pledges, which had plagued a previous drive, the committee had arranged that the subscribers would pay six percent interest on any unpaid balance! For any foreseeable future, the success of this drive ended the seminary's financial problems. Now, as one report had it, the congregations of the Reformed Church would no longer be asked to contribute to the cause of theological education but would be free to make their gifts to the missionary work of the denomination. That attitude which seemed eminently right at the time was to plague the seminary in years to come. For the moment, however, the relief from financial stringency enabled the synod to appropriate the sum of $200 a year for the purchase of new books for the library.

The financial euphoria produced by the success of the 1835 fund drive was followed by a spiritual one as well. Soon after the seminary had moved to New Brunswick under Dr. Livingston's leadership, an interest in foreign missions[11] had developed in the student body and had resulted in the formation in 1811 of the Berean Society, the ancestor of the present Society of Inquiry. The rise of the missionary movement in the Reformed Church had found a congenial response at New Brunswick. David Abeel, the pioneer missionary to China, often visited his old school to plead for volunteers. In the fall of 1836 four recent graduates of the seminary, Elihu Doty (1836), Jacob Ennis (1835), Elbert Nevius (1834), and William Youngblood (1835), with their families, all set sail for Borneo as missionaries. Because of the influence of Abeel they had volunteered for service in China, but when it was found that that was politically impossible, the group expressed its willingness to go to Borneo where a new mission was opened under the sponsorship of the American Board of Commissioners.

But the missionary volunteers were only part of what seemed to be widespread religious revival. The entering class in the seminary in 1837 numbered sixteen, the largest in the history of the institution to that date. All but two of the new students were Rutgers graduates, which indicated that the revival had had a marked effect on the college. One can only wonder, incidentally, what connections there were between this revival and the terrible financial crash of 1837, the worst in the country's history up to that point. Evidently the fathers of the church thought that there

David Abeel

were real relationships. Reporting to the synod of 1838, the Committee on the State of Religion had this to say.

> When every wish appeared to be gratified and every hope to be realized, our great commercial metropolis was touched in the very seat of her pride and greatness, and the instability of all earthly grandeur and the certainty how soon riches may take to themselves wings and fly away was fully demonstrated, when the devouring element in a few hours consumed the palaces of our merchant princes and the rich productions of every quarter of the globe.
>
> The Lord laid his hands on the products of our fertile lands—a land which had always hitherto supplied the wants of her children refused her bounties. These, combining with other causes, have produced in many minds an entire conviction of the truth, "the Lord omnipotent reigneth."[12]

In spite of the success of the college as a feeder to the seminary, however, the synod of 1839 was an explosive one. What had been growing dissatisfaction with the administrative skills of

Dr. Milledoler now came to a head, especially since Dr. Janeway who had served as vice president had resigned in 1838 and was evidently unwilling to reconsider his decision. A move to relieve Milledoler of his presidential office was narrowly turned back, and a substitute motion had been made calling for the appointment of a special committee to meet with the Rutgers trustees and to decide "the best mode of abrogating or modifying the Covenant."

That committee reported to a special session of synod the next month. Dr. Milledoler had been deeply wounded by the previous synodical actions and had submitted his resignation as president of the college to the Rutgers trustees. Taking note of that fact, the special committee recommended that "no theological professor shall hereafter be the president of the College" and accepted the recommendation of the trustees that Dr. John Ludlow should be named to the post at a salary of $2,500 per annum, provided that a special fund of $40,000 be raised, the income of which was to be used for the president's salary.

By 1840 it was evident that the efforts to raise this fund had been a disastrous failure. Not only was the financial situation of the country still an uncertain one, but the major sources of money in the Reformed Church were controlled by the party called "ultra," which was certainly not going to contribute to the cause of Dr. Milledoler's chief opponent. It must have given members of the traditional party a good deal of silent glee to hear at the synod of 1840 that there was simply no support for the enthusiastic triumph of the Ludlowites the previous year.

But Dr. Milledoler's troubles were not ended. Although no longer facing the trials and tribulations of a college president, he was facing at least a minor revolution among the seminary students. Twenty-six members of the middler and senior classes had presented a complaint to the Board of Superintendents in May of 1841 about Professor Milledoler's teaching. The substance of their complaint was that he used a woefully outdated textbook, Marck's *Medulla,* a seventeenth-century compendium of scholastic Reformed theology, and that he required his students to commit large parts of it to memory. There had been rumors of this dissatisfaction for several years, but since nothing happened, the students had decided to take matters into their own hands. (The twenty-six complainants represented the total enrollment of the two classes and included names of young men who were to become celebrated in their later ministry.)

The General Synod had never before received a student petition and obviously did not know how to deal with it. While refusing to entertain the document, it had to acknowledge that there was trouble in the department of didactic theology and appointed a committee to investigate. The committee was to have power to require any alterations in the teaching style which it deemed necessary.

The committee met soon after its appointment and, taking its assignment seriously, after consultation with both students and professor, drew up suggestions for some radical changes in the course of instruction in the theological department. Such suggestions were entirely unacceptable to Dr. Milledoler who tendered his resignation to a special meeting of the synod in September of 1841. Heartily weary of the whole affair, synod voted to accept the resignation and proceeded to elect as Milledoler's successor Dr. John Ludlow, who once more refused the invitation to come to New Brunswick Seminary.

Dr. Milledoler's resignation marked the end of an era in the life of both college and seminary. Already relieved of his duties as college president, he was succeeded in that office not by Dr. Ludlow, who had evidently over-reached himself, but by Abraham Bruyn Hasbrouck, a layman from Kingston, New York. After Dr. Milledoler's resignation as theological professor was accepted, it must have been bitter medicine for him to know that synod's first choice for his successor here was also Dr. Ludlow.

The obvious conclusion is that poor Dr. Milledoler had outlived his time. Sixty-six years of age at the time of his resignation, he was still an eighteenth-century rational supernaturalist. After all, he had been ordained in 1794! He was simply unable to understand the new world of the nineteenth century. Dr. Ludlow, with whom Milledoler and his party had tangled so often, was certainly no wild-eyed radical, but he was open to some of the new currents of both criticism and evangelicalism which were beginning to influence the American church.

While it was not the style of the time to make public comment about ecclesiastical disputes, it is not difficult to read between the lines of the following encomium.

> He [Dr. Ludlow] was honest as the day and as generous as he was honest. He chose ever the most liberal policy and inclined to the most charitable judgment. . . . He was vigorous when controversy demanded and resolute in urging sound policy, despite of opposing minds; and he could not, therefore, avoid some rude shocks and sharp assaults.[13]

V

The Fading of the Covenant

The Covenant between Rutgers and the seminary finally agreed on in 1840, though no one recognized it at the time, paved the way for the ultimate separation of the two institutions. The changes seemed minor; the synod still retained ownership of the college property, and the theological professors still did duty as part-time members of the college faculty. The biggest change was that no theological professor was to serve as president of the college. Although the implications had to be worked out, the Covenant of 1840 gave the trustees much wider responsibilities in operating Rutgers. Except for a general oversight, the synod would henceforth confine its attention to the operation of the seminary.

The first task faced by the synod after Milledoler's resignation and Ludlow's refusal to accept the nomination was the choice of a new professor of theology. Another special synod meeting was called for October of 1841 at which the Rev. Dr. Samuel A. Van Vranken, minister of the Broome Street Church in New York, then one of the leading congregations in the city, was chosen professor of didactic and polemic theology. At first Dr. Van Vranken made it a condition of his acceptance that he be relieved of teaching responsibilities in the college, but a compromise was effected by which he would do no college teaching until he had completed the lectures for his theological instruction.

Fifty years old at the time of his election, Dr. Van Vranken had attended Union College for three years and then had had to leave because of financial reverses in the family. Graduated from New Brunswick Seminary in the class of 1817, he had served several congregations in the Reformed Church before his election to the professorate in 1841. Van Vranken's theological loyalties in the dispute-ridden Reformed Church have been described by one of his students.

His life-long bosom friend was Dr. Ludlow—classmate and colleague—classmate in College and Seminary—and colleague also in Seminary and College.[1]

For the next decade there were no changes in the seminary faculty. The trio of Cannon, McClelland, and Van Vranken remained together as a faculty, and the seminary seemed to have entered an era of peace.

Student enrollment during the decade remained fairly constant, averaging between thirty and thirty-five. The only minor flap to occur in the first part of the decade concerned an 1843 recommendation for a public seminary commencement. The Board of Superintendents felt, and the Committee on Professorate concurred, that it would be a fine thing if a public service was held at which the members of the graduating class gave prepared discourses from memory, followed by an address by one of the faculty. Apparently such an exercise was held in 1844 in the newly-formed Second Reformed Church in New Brunswick. The attending audience was made up mostly of townspeople and college and seminary friends of the graduates. The graduates found the preparation for the occasion burdensome, and the fact that the college commencement was only a few days away cut into the size of the audience. All things considered, it was decided that commencement was not a happy experiment and the synod of 1845 voted to discontinue it.

These were years which saw the coming of the railroad to New Brunswick and the same synod of 1845 was reminded that the educational property could no longer be allowed to remain in such shabby condition.

By construction of the railroad communication through New Brunswick, our institution is brought to the border of one of the greatest thoroughfares in our country and we cannot but realize in consequence the importance of making its whole appearance attractive to the many thousands who in the course of a year fix their gaze on it.[2]

Specifically, the committee listed such items as repairing the street in front of the campus and the fences surrounding it. Though nobody looking from a train window could see the improvements, the committee went on to include repainting the library cases, replacing the chapel floor, and fixing leaks in the roof. Of the 5,000 volumes in the library, many were in need of rebinding, and a catalogue of the library's holdings was desperately needed. All of these requests were authorized by the synod which, to help with the costs, ordered that each student in both Rutgers and the seminary be charged one dollar per year for the use of the library.

Matters continued in this placid state for the rest of the decade. The cessation of strife between college and seminary gave their combined boards opportunity to work on the library. A librarian was appointed in 1846 in the person of Charles Romondt, a graduate of both Rutgers and the seminary. At the time of the library's removal to the newly-constructed Van Nest Hall in 1849, Romondt estimated that it contained 10,000 volumes, many of them "rare and valuable." He promised to work on the catalogue which had been proposed in 1845, but its publication was delayed until 1847 for lack of the necessary funding.

Something did occur in 1847 which was to have a far-reaching effect on the life of the seminary, but it was hardly noticed at the time. The first official recognition of it came in a report of the Committee on Missions to the General Synod of June, 1847.

> A new body of pilgrims has reached our shores from Holland, the land of our fathers, and the shelter in ages gone by to outcasts by persecution. The movement will not lose on the score of its moral grandeur by comparison with any associated act of emigration in the history of our country. . . . Providence has cast the lot of the first detachment in the immediate vicinity of our Western churches.[3]

It would take some years before the impact of this second Dutch immigration was fully felt in the seminary, but it would prove to be a very considerable influence.

The first break in the placid state set in the 1840s came in 1851 with the resignation of Professor McClelland. In ill health for some time, he found his additional duties as sole teacher of Hebrew, ancient geography, and antiquities more than he could take and proposed an extended visit to Europe as the cure for his maladies. Three candidates were proposed to the synod as his successor, and the election was won by Dr. William H. Campbell, principal of the Albany Academy. This choice was, eventually, to change the entire picture of both college and seminary.

A native of Baltimore, Maryland, and a graduate of Dickenson College and Princeton Seminary, Dr. Campbell had served as both a pastor and an educator before coming to New Brunswick, having served as principal of Erasmus Hall in Flatbush as well as of the Albany Academy. Dr. McClelland's resignation in 1851 was followed in 1852 by that of Dr. Cannon. Now a man of seventy-six with rapidly-failing health, he had suffered an almost complete loss of speech. In accepting his resignation synod named him professor emeritus and voted to continue to pay his full salary. Dr. McClelland, however, lived only a few months after his resignation.

In seeking for a successor, the synod of 1852 once again turned to Dr. John Ludlow, offering him the chair of church history, pastoral theology, and church government. This time Dr. Ludlow saw fit to accept the invitation, resign his post as provost of the

William H. Campbell

University of Pennsylvania, and return to New Brunswick. The atmosphere had changed completely from the earlier days when he had refused one invitation after another. Gone was the rigid control of the "ultra" party. With his old friend Van Vranken as one of his colleagues and the imaginative and creative Campbell as another, Ludlow obviously believed that New Brunswick at last could be a congenial place.

The library continued to attract attention and support. In 1852 Rensselaer Westerlo, a son of the distinguished eighteenth-century Albany domine, bequeathed his father's library of 250 volumes of Dutch theology to New Brunswick. His example was cited to encourage others who might have similar collections to make them available to the institutions in New Brunswick.

The changing constituency of the Reformed Church was evidenced by the fact that the entering class of 1853 contained three German-speaking students (another was already enrolled as a middler) who "will be duly furnished for preaching the Gospel in their own language to this numerous and interesting class of our extending population." The entering class of 1854 contained two more German students as well as a third who was spending a probationary year in New Brunswick. This same entering class enrolled the first student from the Netherlands.

Tradition has it that Dr. Campbell found the situation of two institutions sharing a common building to be intolerable and urged his students to complain about it. Whether or not he was directly responsible, from 1854 the topic became a question for lively discussion. Students and faculty alike met with the superintendents that year, who reported on the meetings to the synod of 1855. The students called the board's attention to such facts as the cost of private accommodations in New Brunswick since there was no student housing available. They claimed that five students had already chosen to attend other seminaries where better provision was made for their living arrangements. The faculty strongly suggested a separate library and facilities for separate lecture rooms and social halls. Obviously the problem had to be faced.

A special committee of faculty, students, and superintendents, chaired by Professor Van Vranken, had discovered that the average cost of board and room at New Brunswick was $3 to $3.50 per week. At Princeton and Union seminaries in New York, both of which maintained theological halls, the cost ranged from $1.45 to $1.90. The committee saw no other solution but the erection of a theological hall which would contain dormitories, a refectory, and public rooms. But where would the money to pay for such a building come from?

The Committee on Education, headed by the celebrated Dr. George Washington Bethune, to which the whole question had been referred, thought it had the answer—the consistory of the Collegiate Church in New York! That consistory had just recently given $25,000 to the College Endowment Fund. Preliminary inquiries seemed to indicate a willingness to make the same contribution to the proposed theological hall, the total cost of which was estimated at $40,000. The committee even knew a suitable location, a vacant lot on Somerset Street, owned by the seminary's old friend, Abraham Van Nest.

To those who had suggested an alternate scheme, one of subsidizing the cost of living in New Brunswick (which the Collegiate consistory had done in 1855 to the tune of $700), the committee had a ready reply. Over the long term, the cost of erecting and maintaining a theological hall would be cheaper. The experience of both Princeton and Union demonstrated this. At Princeton, where the commons were considered to be poorly run, the savings came to a dollar a week per student, while at Union it was two dollars per week. That kind of subsidy would involve the annual income on $60,000, instead of the $25,000 for which the committee was asking.

With such logic the committee persuaded the synod to go forward with the construction of a theological hall and to appoint a committee which had power to act, as soon as $25,000 was available from the Collegiate consistory or from any other source. Such a committee was appointed consisting of the three professors, Dr. Talbot Chambers, one of the Collegiate ministers, the

Rev. Thomas Strong of Flatbush, and Dr. Bethune. Dr. Campbell
had been part of the institution for a mere three years, but he
had certainly produced results!

The General Synod which met in special session in New York
in October of 1855 must have been one of the most exciting in
the history of the church. The first report was from the Board of
Superintendents and was dated as of their meetings of July 17.
They reported the sad news that the Collegiate consistory was
unwilling to make the $25,000 gift and had even revoked its
annual student subsidy.

A bright prospect is thus unhappily blighted and the sad consequences will fall heavily, we fear, on those now in course of preparation for the ministry in our institutions; while it must for the present
diminish the number of those who would otherwise have sought admission to them.[4]

The superintendents could do little else but throw up their hands
and hope for the best some time in the future.

It was now the turn of the special committee for which Professor Van Vranken reported. Brushing aside the request to the
Collegiate consistory to which the committee had received no
official answer, Professor Van Vranken announced the gift of
$30,000 from Mrs. Ann Hertzog of Philadelphia for the erection
of the Peter Hertzog Theological Hall in memory of her husband.
The committee further reported that plots of ground extending
from George Street to College Avenue and valued at between
$15,000 and $16,000 had been given by Col. James Neilson,
Mr. David Bishop, and Mr. Charles Dayton. Along the whole
front of these grounds, the Common Council of the City of New
Brunswick had plans for an eighty-foot-wide street which would
probably be known as Neilson Avenue.

On the basis of these gifts and the authority granted it by the
General Synod, the committee had approved plans and let con-
tracts. The new Hertzog Theological Hall was to be ready for
occupancy by September 1, 1856. The committee, in fact, invited

all members of synod to attend the laying of the cornerstone on
November 8!

What happened obviously was that Philadelphia had been persuaded to supply what New York had rejected. Early along in its
deliberations, the committee had decided that the Collegiate
Church consistory would not respond favorably to the synod's
request. As is apparent from Dr. Van Vranken's report, they did
not wait for a formal refusal, but assuming that their private information (from Dr. Chambers?) was correct, went in search of
other sources. Both Dr. Bethune and Dr. Ludlow knew Mrs.
Hertzog well. Dr. Bethune had been her pastor for many years
and understood that she intended to leave $25,000 to the semi-
nary to endow a chair in her husband's memory. Her two old
friends persuaded her to increase the amount to $30,000 and to
give it immediately for an urgently-needed cause. The New
Brunswick gentlemen who gave the land were good friends of
both Rutgers and the seminary, and an additional $2,000 for more
real estate was obtained from the Wessells brothers in Paramus,

Ann Hertzog

New Jersey. Admittedly it was a high-powered committee, but it was in business for only four months—and Hertzog Hall was on its way!

Dedication services for the new building were held on September 23, 1856. The facility stood on a hill at the extreme edge of town "in the midst of desolateness," as a committee report stated. Landscaping and fencing were soon added and the committee which had raised the funds for the building also took responsibility for furnishing it. Donations made toward the furnishings ranged from one of $500 from Stephen Van Rensselaer of Albany to one of $2.50 from a "young lady of Poughkeepsie." While no women's auxiliary yet existed, the committee had secured gifts from the ladies of twelve congregations. Not to be forgotten were the young churches of Overisel, Graafschap, and Zeeland, Michigan, which contributed $3.35, $3.09, and $18.70 respectively toward the cost of furnishing the new building.

The joy of having Hertzog Hall as the home of the theological seminary was overshadowed, however, by the long illness of Professor Ludlow, whose death occurred on September 8, 1857. More than anyone else he was responsible for Mrs. Hertzog's gift, but he only lived to enjoy the result of that gift for a very short time. A special meeting of synod, held in October of 1857, chose Dr. Bethune to take his place, but that gifted pulpit orator, realizing that his place was not in a theological seminary, declined. Samuel Merrill Woodbridge, a graduate of New York University and New Brunswick Seminary and pastor of the Second Church in New Brunswick, was then chosen for the post and began a tenure that lasted for forty-four years, the longest in the history of the school.

With the opening of Hertzog Hall in 1856, the unraveling of the Covenant was just a question of time. Each institution now had its own building, although the apartments in the college building were still used to house theological faculty and their families. The libraries were being divided and the theological collection was housed in a room in the new theological hall. Seminary faculty still had some responsibilities for college teaching,

Hertzog Hall

but these were decreasing gradually. The General Synod still had
title to the buildings of Rutgers, as well as that of the seminary,
and initially at least resisted any attempt to transfer title back to
the Rutgers trustees.

A visitor to New Brunswick at the time would have been impressed by the two large buildings, rather similar in style, which
crowned two hills. Between them there was absolutely nothing
but a long meadow, bounded on either side by George Street
and College Avenue. A new president's house and Van Nest Hall
flanked the old college building along Somerset Street; Hertzog
Hall stood in solitary splendor on its hill which soon came to be
known locally as "Holy Hill."

As can be seen from the discussion about board and room that
took place before the building of Hertzog Hall, Princeton and
Union seminaries were the models which the New Brunswick
superintendents set for themselves, largely because they had
proved the most competitive. Andover was probably too far away,
and divinity schools such as those of Harvard and Yale were in

a very different kind of situation. By this time both Princeton and Union had a full-time faculty of four while the New Brunswick faculty consisted of only three. As early as October of 1857 the Committee on Professorate recommended that the synod explore the possibility of creating a fourth chair in the faculty, a professorship of sacred rhetoric. Realizing that such a proposal would involve long-term planning, the same committee recommended that a lectureship in pulpit eloquence be established, to be filled by one of the most eloquent pulpiteers of the day, the same Dr. Bethune who had just refused to accept the chair of ecclesiastical history, pastoral theology, and church government. For his services, Dr. Bethune was promised a sum of $700, plus $30 for traveling expenses.

Dr. Bethune accepted the offer and during the next year spent one day each week at the seminary. To have secured the services of one of America's best-known preachers for this lectureship was something like a stroke of genius. In a report to the synod of 1858 Bethune outlined his course, which provides a fascinating picture of what must have been one of the first classes in homiletics offered in any seminary.

> After an introductory lecture, I read, at proper intervals, five others to the assembled classes on
> 1. Utterance
> 2. Articulation
> 3. Intonation
> 4. Emphasis
> 5. Gesture
>
> Besides these, I gave extemporaneous, though not unpremeditated advices to the several classes on various subjects intimately connected with the public service of the Church; and also spent much time in criticizing the reading of the students in Scripture and hymns.
>
> For this purpose, after the first few weeks, I met the students in the Second Church, its use having been kindly accorded to us. This allowed the student to ascend the pulpit and exercise his voice in a larger audience chamber.[5]

George Washington Bethune

The visiting lecturer went on to point out that owing to railroad schedules he had spent between ten and eleven hours on each visit to the seminary, including his three hours of teaching! No offer was apparently made to continue his lectureship, but that may very well have been because Dr. Bethune had indicated an unwillingess to give that much time, given his busy church schedule and extensive outside lecturing. It may also have been due to the sorry fact that he had not been paid the amount promised him. The committee which had been appointed to arrange for Dr. Bethune's services reported that four members of the committee had raised $498.90 while the other three members of the committee had done nothing. The special committee appointed to purchase part of the late Dr. Ludlow's library had done better (probably because Dr. Campbell was its chairman); they had raised the entire $600 necessary for their purpose. Unfortunately, Dr. Bethune had to wait until June of 1859 before he received full compensation for his lectureship.

Such difficulty pretty much dampened the earlier enthusiasm for a fourth professorship. Actually, the seminary was operating at a small deficit each year as it was, and it was obvious to all concerned that, desirable as it was, New Brunswick was not yet ready to play in the same league as Union or Princeton with a fourth professorship, barring, of course, the unexpected gift of some "opulent member."

One of the problems which continued to plague the Board of Superintendents during these years was that of student preaching. Time and again the synod ordered that students were not to preach in congregations except under the strict supervision of a member of the faculty and with his expressed permission. Time and again the board had to report that the rule seemed unenforceable. To the synod of 1860, for example, the board reported that all but two members of the senior class had violated the rule, as well as seven middlers. Their names were listed as transgressors, but no other penalties were given.

Since the number of transgressions had been eleven in 1859, and twenty-one in 1860, the Committee on Professorate decided to crack down. In rather acid terms, the committee described the situation.

> If the members of the Seminary be *preachers,* they are no longer *students.* And if they be *students,* they are not *preachers.* It is true that the popular gaze is of late sometimes called to fix itself on *boy preachers.* But if we acknowledge such precocity, it would be rather as the exception than the rule. . . . Your committee believes that this unlicensed licensure and the constitution of our Theological courses of training for the pulpit and pastorship are absolutely incompatible.[6]

With that reasoning as its background, the committee recommended that future violation of the rules be grounds for suspension from the seminary. Its recommendation carried by a vote of sixty-three to thirty-five.

The fact that thirty-five members of the synod voted against the recommendation is a pretty good indication of a rising tide of opinion in the church that the old rules were no longer adequate for a new day. How much, for example, had Dr. Bethune's lectures in pulpit eloquence been responsible for the rapid rise in violations of the rule? How can one justify giving young men special training in homiletics and then allowing them no chance to put it into practice? Obviously the synod had not yet heard the end of this question.

The whole question of enlarging the faculty had to be deferred because of two removals from the present faculty which occurred in fairly close succession. On New Year's Day, 1861, Professor Van Vranken died in his sixty-ninth year. The following June, the synod elected as his successor the Rev. Joseph F. Berg, pastor of the Second Reformed Church in Philadelphia. Dr. Berg came to the seminary from a very colorful and lively background. Born in the West Indies to Danish Moravian missionary parents, his entire training had been in Moravian institutions in England. He had come to this country in 1825 for further training for the Moravian ministry, but in a few years he had joined the German Reformed Church and was ordained by that church in 1835.

During his ministry in the First German Reformed Church in Philadelphia Dr. Berg had also studied medicine at Jefferson Medical College, from which he received the degree of doctor of medicine. It was also during his Philadelphia ministry that he had become increasingly agitated by the liturgical and sacramental theology of Mercersburg Seminary. In 1852 he came to the conclusion that he was battling the Mercersburg professors almost single-handedly in the German Reformed Church, which became known as the Second Reformed Dutch Church of Philadelphia where he had enjoyed considerable success.

The most severe loss to the faculty came two years later when Dr. Campbell was elected president of Rutgers College, resigning his professorship at the synod of 1863. The first man chosen to succeed him was the Rev. Hervey Ganse, pastor of the Northwest Church in New York and one of the rising stars of the metropolitan pulpit. When he declined (probably for much the same reasons as Dr. Bethune), the synod turned to the Rev. John De Witt, pastor of the Church in Millstone, New Jersey, and a son of the beloved Professor De Witt of an earlier time. John De Witt had come to New Brunswick as a small child and had grown up with both college and seminary. A man of forty-two when he joined the seminary faculty, he made many rich contributions in future years.

Once Dr. Campbell had become president of Rutgers, he lost no time in severing the last bonds of the Covenant. Because of his reputation in the Reformed Church, he easily persuaded the synod of 1864 to deed the college property back to Rutgers trustees and surrender all interest in it. The sum of $12,000 was agreed upon as adequate recompense for the money which the synod had paid for the building in 1823 and for other capital expenses over the years. Seminary faculty were allowed to continue to live in the building until new quarters could be provided for them on the seminary's new location. Members of the seminary faculty were excused from further teaching in the college, with the exception of Dr. Berg who was required to teach theology at Rutgers in the terms of the original Covenant of 1807. By mutual consent that Covenant was abrogated in 1867 and the two institutions were at last totally separate. The college faculty described the situation this way:

> [It] certainly is a subject of congratulation that these two institutions which in their early history like two ships had to be lashed together for mutual safety and could command only the divided labor of the same crew have been so enlarged and strengthened as to move on independently and to demand individual labors.[7]

After 1867 the seminary had something it had never had previously—three professors devoting full time to their theological labors. The college had full independence and the total use of its historic building, although the deed of reconveyance from the synod in 1864 required that the president and three-quarters of

the Board of Trustees must always be communicant members of
the Dutch Reformed Church.

The Covenant had not died a violent death; bit by bit it had
simply faded away. Each school was now free to face the future
with its own resources. The fact is that for both institutions the
Covenant had outlived its usefulness. So far as the college was
concerned, the post-Civil War era was to see an enormous expansion of secular university education of which no college could
take advantage if it remained the undergraduate department of
a theological school. President Campbell and his colleagues, Professors Cook and Murray, were already anxious to take advantage
of the provisions of the Morrill Act which the New Jersey legislature had accepted in 1863. "Will Rutgers College be the al-
moner of this government munificence or will she stand back and
see it put into less safe and capable hands?" So began the association of the college with the State of New Jersey which in years
to come was completely to transform the life of the school.

Nor could the seminary have afforded much longer to share
both faculty and facilities with the college. Theological education
was on the threshold of a new era in which specialization and
scholarship were increasingly to become the order of the day. A
faculty which had to devote nearly half its time to undergraduate
education could never qualify for full recognition in the new
world of theological education.

It was the end of an era when the last seminary professor
moved out of his apartment in Old Queens and left Rutgers free
to use the building for new classroom space. In many ways that
era had been helpful for both institutions, but the time had now
arrived for each institution to face a strange new world, painful
as the experience of maturing in such a world might be.

VI

The Golden Age

The record of New Brunswick Seminary during the first decade after its removal to its own premises in Hertzog Hall scarcely reveals that the American Civil War was fought during this period. Part of the reason for this strange fact is that in the years before the firing on Fort Sumter, the southern cause enjoyed considerable popularity in the Reformed Church in America. One of the chief defenses of slavery, *Slaveholding not Sinful*, was written in 1853 by Dr. Samuel Blanchard How, pastor of the First Reformed Church in New Brunswick. Slavery had in fact continued longer in Reformed Church areas such as Bergen County, New Jersey, and Kings County, Long Island, than in most part of the Northeast.

The most compelling reason for this attitude, however, was the heavy investment which New York bankers and merchants had in the southern states. As David McCullough has pointed out,

> . . . the South owed the banks, merchants, and mill owners of New York and Brooklyn nearly $200,000,000 which would be forfeited if there was war. The South was also the major market for goods shipped from New York Harbor, and Southerners were the chief buyers of Brooklyn-made carriages and harnesses. On both sides of the East River factories produced cheap cotton cloth "exclusively for the southern trade."[1]

In view of such circumstances, it is not surprising that even after the outbreak of hostilities, a motion to support the government carried in the General Synod of June, 1861, only by a vote of seventy-one to thirty-four!

Nor was seminary enrollment greatly affected by the outbreak

of hostilities. There were fifty-seven students the year before the
Civil War broke out; there were forty-eight during the year that
it ended. Only two students, Brandt and Van Doren, left the
seminary to enlist in the Union army, and both returned in a
relatively short time to finish their course. There is obviously no
way of estimating the number of students who *might* have come
to the seminary if military service had not called them away, or
how many of those never came because their military experience
had changed their minds about their call to the ministry.

During these years of bitter conflict, New Brunswick Seminary
seems pretty much to have engaged in business as usual. The
chief topic of conversation on Holy Hill was not Gettysburg or
Sherman's march to the sea but how to provide for a fourth
member of the faculty, especially in the area of pastoral theology.
The question had first been raised in 1857 when Dr. Bethune's
lectureship had been accepted as a temporary measure. The year
1857, however, was a terrible time during which to raise money,
since it was the time of a financial panic in the country almost as
bad as that of 1837. Then came the Civil War years, with all of
their financial uncertainty. The possibility of raising enough money
to support a fourth faculty member seemed unlikely.

In 1864 the Standing Committee on Hertzog Hall received
word from the Rev. Dr. Nicholas E. Smith, pastor of the Middle
Dutch Church in Brooklyn, that he was willing to pledge $40,000
toward the cost of increasing the faculty to four on two conditions:
one, that the churches would contribute an additional $40,000,
and that the salaries of the faculty members would be raised to
$2,500 a year. Faculty salaries had been set at $1,800 for many
years, but the terrible inflation of the Civil War had rendered
that amount pitifully inadequate.

The three members of the faculty, Professors Berg, De Witt,
and Woodbridge, took up Dr. Smith's challenge and canvassed
the church thoroughly. Dr. De Witt took leadership in the drive,
enlisting the enthusiastic support of the Hudson River Ministerial
Association. As a result of these strenuous efforts, more than
$48,000 was raised to meet Dr. Smith's offer of a matching gift

(on which he was paying the seminary annual interest). The synod of 1865 was jubilant.

> [It] introduces a new era in the history of our Theological Seminary, providing for its expansion in raising up a larger number of pious and better trained young men for the Christian ministry, just as this great crisis in our country and the American Church, when, in addition to previously existing missionary fields, the whole South in its utter moral destitution is laid at our feet, appealing for our sympathies, prayers and labors for the salvation of its entire population, white and colored. The wonderful Providence of God has crowned with success the efforts to raise eighty thousand dollars . . . just at the time when this vast field, white to the harvest, lies outspread before our eyes.[2]

Dr. David D. Demarest, pastor of the Dutch Church in Hudson, New York, was chosen professor of pastoral theology and sacred rhetoric, and his salary and that of his three colleagues was set at $2,500 per year each.

The abrogation of the Covenant meant that the seminary also had to make provision for housing the members of the faculty, since the apartments in Old Queens were being surrendered to the Rutgers trustees. The same synod of 1865 which had received the good news about the fourth professorship authorized the building of three professorial residences on the same grounds as Hertzog Hall, at a total cost not to exceed $40,000. These homes were to be "of sufficient size to accommodate large families and in a suitable style of architecture with corresponding improvements." Since the building committee had in hand $22,000, $12,000 of which had come from the sale of Old Queens to the Rutgers trustees, it was authorized to raise the necessary balance from the church.

The library was at the same time greatly enhanced by the gift of the theological and classical library of the late Dr. Bethune. His widow made the gift on condition that the name *Bethune* be clearly stamped on each volume. Since Dr. Bethune had been

one of America's first bibliophiles, the 2,000 volumes which were
added in this way not only crowded the library room in Hertzog
Hall but gave the collection a core of rare and valuable volumes.
Mrs. Bethune later presented a marble bust of her late husband
for the library.

Everyone was sure that New Brunswick Seminary had at last
come into its own. The faculty now numbered four, with salaries
that were at least competitive. Three new faculty residences were
being built on Holy Hill; the first was ready for occupancy in
1866, the other two were completed by 1868. Thanks to the
generosity of Mrs. Bethune and other donors, the library was
gaining in both quantity and quality. The post-war years seemed
to be the most promising that the seminary had ever known.

The euphoria dissipated quickly when it was learned in 1867
that Dr. Smith was simply unable to meet his pledge of $40,000
and asked to be released from it. Financial reverses had made
what was to have been the most generous single gift in the seminary's history impossible. Apparently Smith had invested his
money in oil and what had promised to be a bonanza turned out
to be a failure.[3] It has to be said, however, that his promise of
a matching gift, though never fulfilled, had spurred the Reformed
Church to greater activity on behalf of the seminary than had
been seen in many years.

To meet the crisis, the synod of 1868 appointed a special committee of nine persons, all laymen, and one professor to raise
$100,000 for the seminary endowment. Probably because it had
seen previous seminary fund-raising drives falter, the Board of
Direction asked to be associated with the effort. The first move
made by the new joint committee proved to be one of the most
strategic in the history of the seminary. The committee asked the
Rev. Dr. James Alexander Hervey Cornell to serve as its agent.
Dr. Cornell accepted and began his work in 1869. If ever there
has been an unsung hero in the history of New Brunswick Seminary it is James A. H. Cornell.

A graduate of both Rutgers College and New Brunswick Seminary (class of 1841), Dr. Cornell had served several pastorates

James A. H. Cornell

in the Reformed Church, finally accepting the secretaryship of its Board of Education in 1856. He served for five years and then resigned, owing to the inability of the board to meet his salary. Cornell retired to the little Hudson Valley village of New Baltimore, New York, which had been the scene of one of his first pastorates. He was living there in semi-retirement when the invitation came to act as fund-raising agent for the seminary.[4]

It was during his Board of Education days that Dr. Cornell had first come to know James Suydam, a retired New York dry goods merchant who had become a successful speculator in New York real estate and held numerous directorships in city banks and insurance companies. Suydam was also an active member of

the Middle Collegiate Church in New York. Since Dr. Cornell
had previously been able to share in Suydam's philanthropy, he
was the first person to whom he went with the seminary's problem once he had been appointed agent (or as we would say today,
"fund raiser" or "development officer").

The synod of 1869 received the good news that Mr. Suydam
had donated $40,000 to endow a professorship

> to be called and always hereafter known as the James Suydam Pro-
> fessorship of Didactic and Polemic Theology in the Theological Sem-
> inary of the Reformed Church in America.[5]

It was probably equally delighted to learn that this $40,000 was
not a pledge but had already been paid in United States bonds!

Later in the same year Dr. Cornell approached both Mr. Suydam and a new acquaintance, Gardner Sage, about another seminary problem. Sage, a civil surveyor and engineer who had laid
out many of the newer streets in the city of New York as well as
executed Olmstead's plans for Central Park, was a somewhat
newer member of the Washington Square Church whose pastor,
Dr. Mancius S. Hutton, had undoubtedly introduced him to
Cornell.

This time the problem concerned faculty housing. When provisions were made for professorial residences after the relinquish-
ing of the Old Queens apartments, the faculty numbered only
three. Accordingly, three residences had been built on Holy Hill,
two on the College Avenue side and one on the George Street
side.[6] The faculty now numbered four, and Dr. Berg, the faculty
member who had to rent his own house on Easton Avenue, was
finding the cost exceedingly high.

Across from the seminary, at the corner of George Street, Dr.
George Cook, a Rutgers professor (of agricultural school fame),
had built a splendid stone house soon after he had come to New
Brunswick in 1853. Now, for personal reasons, Professor Cook
wished to dispose of the property. His asking price was $18,000,
and Cornell was able to persuade his friends Suydam and Sage

to donate $9,000 each to make the house available to the seminary as a fourth faculty residence.

Cornell may have been able to relieve the financial concerns of the institution, but in this same period an increasing concern was the falling student enrollment. When the decade opened, the enrollment had been fifty-seven; by the end of the decade it numbered only twenty-three. No one could explain such a rapid decline, especially in view of the attention that had been lavished on faculty and buildings. Some blamed it on the fact that a new department of theological education had been opened at Hope College in Holland, Michigan, in 1867. But since that department never numbered more than nine students, that obviously was not the reason for New Brunswick's decline in student enrollment.

In 1867, when the enrollment had dropped to thirty-four, the superintendents did not seem too alarmed but felt that the trend downward was common in other seminaries. The following year, however, the enrollment had declined to twenty-seven at a time when it was costing the Reformed Church almost $20,000 a year to maintain the seminary. The superintendents pointed out that the school could accommodate several times the number of students at no additional cash outlay. What was the reason for the decline?

Although the superintendents employed somewhat fancy language to answer their own question, they came very close to the real reason—the rapid increase of secularism and materialism in the post-Civil War North.

> . . . The real difficulty lies in the spirit of the age, the declension of self-denying religion, the excessive labors of the ministry and the peculiar condition of the Church. More alluring paths of life lie open on every hand to tempt the untried footsteps of the young, while the uncertainties of his position, the ugly competitions of competing denominations and the prospect of uncared for old age deter the Neophyte from the toilsome stony path of the Heralds of Salvation.[7]

In addition to the fact that in the new industrial North the ministry had to compete with business for recruits in a way that

never before had been true, New Brunswick Seminary had a
peculiar problem of its own. It had to provide everything involved in a first-class theological school for a constituency which
necessarily must be smaller than that of its Congregational or
Presbyterian counterparts. As the 1868 report had indicated, the
basic cost of maintaining an institution for twenty-five students
is basically no different from that of maintaining one for 100.
While the New Brunswick enrollment gradually increased to an
average of approximately forty students, the question continued
to be a nagging one for most of the school's history.

By 1870 student enrollment had fallen to a new low of sixteen,
but the library was continuing to outgrow its very modest quarters in Hertzog Hall. Something had to be done to avoid bibliographical chaos. The ever-ready Dr. Cornell was able to announce
that he had already secured a gift of $35,000 toward the cost of
constructing a new library. The synod felt that a location between
Hertzog Hall and Dr. Demarest's residence (corner of George
Street) would be an appropriate place for the new facility, and
authorized Dr. Cornell to continue to raise money for it.

The first building for which Dr. Cornell was able to raise
money, however, was not a library, although it was to be constructed on the designated library site. James Suydam, it seemed,
had no great interest in libraries, but he was deeply concerned
about student health. He therefore told Dr. Cornell that any new
building in which he might be interested would have to be in the
nature of what today would be called a "student center," the
larger part to be used for a gymnasium in which students could
exercise for their health, while other space could be devoted to
lecture rooms.[8]

Such a building was not exactly the one for which Dr. Cornell
had been looking, but he knew better than to contradict James
Suydam, especially when approximately $100,000 was at stake.
The donor became fascinated with his new project, secured the
services of Henry Hardenbergh, a well-known New York architect, to draw plans for exactly the kind of building he wanted,

deposited bonds to the amount of $50,000 to guarantee his intention to build, and by 1871 was ready to proceed.

Before the building was begun, however, there was another change in the faculty. Dr. Berg, who had served as professor of theology for the past ten years, died on July 20, 1871, after an illness of several months. A special meeting of synod therefore was called for September 27 to choose a successor. The choice was a surprising one: the Rev. Dr. William G. T. Shedd, a Presbyterian minister who was on the faculty of Union Seminary in New York. It is impossible to say at this late date what led the synod to look in this direction. It is possible that because this was

Suydam Hall

now the James Suydam Chair of Theology, the seminary's great benefactor had made the suggestion.

In any event Dr. Shedd did not immediately decline the invitation but asked for time to consider it. Only after repeated interviews and careful thought did Dr. Shedd decide to remain in New York. Since no successor to Dr. Berg could then be chosen before June of 1872, Dr. Woodbridge, professor of church history, was asked to fill in for the year with instruction in theology. For this, he received an extra compensation of $350.

The synod of 1872 filled the vacancy left by Dr. Berg by electing Dr. Abraham Van Zandt, pastor of the Old Brick Church in Montgomery, New York. Although pastor of a large rural congregation at the time of his election, Dr. Van Zandt had formerly been pastor of the Central Reformed Church in New York City where James Suydam had been one of his parishioners. Suydam's pleasure at the election of his former pastor to his chair of theology is evidenced by the fact that he immediately increased the endowment of the chair from $40,000 to $60,000! Whatever may have been his virtues as a teacher (and there is evidence that he represented the more conservative side of the faculty), Dr. Van Zandt's coming to New Brunswick Seminary certainly helped increase its ties to James Suydam!

The special session of General Synod which elected Dr. Van Zandt to the theological chair vacated by the death of Dr. Berg met in the Middle Dutch Church in Brooklyn on September 27, 1871. Every delegate received a special invitation to attend the laying of the cornerstone of the new building. In addition to the gymnasium, the new building contained lecture rooms, a chapel, and a room for the Society of Inquiry, which also contained museum articles brought back by various missionaries.

The building was dedicated on June 5, 1873. This time the General Synod was in session in New Brunswick so there was no problem in getting the delegates to attend. Suydam's old friend, Professor Van Zandt, conducted the dedication service at which four addresses were delivered! A statue of James Suydam, in front of the new building, was unveiled at the same time.

June 5, 1873, was a busy day for New Brunswick Seminary and the General Synod. No sooner had the dedication exercises been completed than the entire company moved to the other side of Hertzog Hall for the laying of the cornerstone of the new Gardner Sage Library—two more addresses! The actual laying of the cornerstone was performed by Dr. Cornell who actually was responsible for persuading Sage to donate the new building. Ever since Suydam had elected to build a student center rather than a library, Cornell had not ceased to worry about the condition of the library in Hertzog Hall. Not only was it terribly overcrowded, but now that it contained Dr. Bethune's valuable collection, the threat of fire was a continuing nightmare.

Apparently Cornell had persuaded Sage to build a new fireproof building for the library about the same time that Suydam decided to build his hall. Sage, however, was much more cautious and hesitant than his friend Suydam. Having accepted the idea in principle, he spent the next two years interviewing architects, investigating various proposals until he finally decided on another New York architect, Detlef Lienau, as the designer of the new library and consented to the 1873 date for the laying of the cornerstone. Obviously, Lienau was influenced in his design for the facade by Hardenbergh's facade for Suydam Hall. Though the two buildings were by no means identical, their facades were sufficiently similar to provide a striking symmetry on either side of Hertzog Hall. The new Gardner Sage Library was ready for dedication on June 4, 1875. Once again the members of General Synod, meeting this time in Jersey City, were in attendance. These dedicatory exercises must have set something of a record. In addition to the dedicatory prayer, seven addresses were given!

Dr. Cornell's influence on Sage and Suydam was not limited to their lifetimes. Suydam's will contained a $20,000 bequest for the upkeep of Suydam Hall, another like amount for the maintenance and improvement of seminary buildings, and a final $20,000 for the erection of the residence for the James Suydam Professor of Theology. (This building, now known as Kooy House, was opened in 1883.) A few years later Gardner Sage left the

Gardner A. Sage Library

seminary the sum of $50,000 to endow a new professorship, without specifying the subject. Between Suydam's death and his own (which occurred in 1882), Sage had given $25,000 to endow Hertzog Hall, $35,000 as an endowment for the library, $20,000 as an endowment for the purchase of new books, $5,000 for finishing the library basement, and $5,000 for scholarships.

Dr. Cornell was not yet finished, however. Although the new library contained many valuable items, it also had many deficiencies which prevented it from being a first-class theological library. Soon after the dedication of the building Cornell raised $35,000 from friends in the Reformed Church to purchase new books for the library. A special committee was appointed, consisting of Dr. Talbot Chambers of the Middle Church in New York, Dr. Chester Hartranft of the Second Reformed Church in New Brunswick, and Dr. Edward Corwin, the well-known Reformed Church historian, who was at that time minister in Millstone, New Jersey, as well as faculty members. With Dr. Cornell's fund, other gifts, and the interest on Sage's endowment, the committee had about $60,000 to spend over the next ten years (1875 to 1885), and it did an excellent job! Officially, Dr. Cornell's position as agent came to an end in 1873 and he returned to the Hudson Valley to pastor the Church in Coeymans, New York. Surely a man who in four years added more than half a million dollars to the seminary's resources in terms of endowments, building, and books deserves more than a mere passing remembrance.

In 1879 the Board of Superintendents decided to try again with a public commencement exercise, to be held on Wednesday evening after the close of school in one of the Reformed churches in New Brunswick. The first such commencement was held on May 18, 1880, in the First Reformed Church. The commencement address was given by Dr. William Ormiston, pastor of the Marble Collegiate Church in New York. Three members of the graduating class of eight gave short presentations, and Dr. Woodbridge, representing the faculty, presented the graduates with their professorial certificates. A final address to the students was

given by Dr. Dwight Bartlett, pastor of the Second Church in
Albany. This time there were no complaints as there had been
some years previously and the May commencement became a
standard feature in the life of the seminary.

Ever since he had undergone serious surgery in 1878, Dr. Van
Zandt had been in poor health, often forced to miss his classes
for several weeks at a time. In 1881 his illness again became
severe and he was unable to function after March. He saw no
alternative than to offer his resignation to the synod which met
in June of that year. (Actually, he died just a few weeks later.)
An effort was made to secure the services of Dr. Chester Hartranft, a member of the faculty of Hartford Seminary and formerly
pastor of the Second Church in New Brunswick. There was great
disappointment when so distinguished an alumnus refused to
leave Hartford. The next choice was Dr. William Augustus Van
Vranken Mabon, who had for the previous thirty-five years been
pastor of the Grove Church in North Bergen, New Jersey. Dr.
Mabon indicated his willingness to assume his duties in December.

On two occasions the synod had sought to secure the services
of faculty members from other seminaries—Dr. Shedd from Union
and Dr. Hartranft from Hartford—and had been refused both
times. There was evidently a desire to break away from the cus-
tom of calling pastors to the professorate, however distinguished
their ministries may have been. That desire reflected the growing
professionalism which was taking place in American theological
education, but at this point New Brunswick was still too small to
take advantage of it. Other seminaries were turning in the direction of graduate schools of theology, while New Brunswick remained a professional school for the training of pastors.

The seminary began its ninety-eighth year in 1882 with a faculty of four. The senior member, Dr. Woodbridge, taught church
history and polity as he had since 1857. Dr. De Witt, the best-
known faculty member outside the Reformed Church, since he
had served as a member of the American Old Testament Revision
Committee since 1872, held the chair of biblical literature. More
widely known within the Reformed Church was Dr. Demarest,

John De Witt (Jr.)

who taught pastoral theology and sacred rhetoric and whose book
*History and Characteristics of the Reformed Protestant Dutch
Church* had enjoyed a wide circulation. Dr. Mabon, the fourth
member of the faculty, had come too recently to have established
a reputation.

Much excitement came in the summer of 1882 with the knowledge that Gardner Sage's will provided $50,000 for the creation
of a fifth professorship at the seminary. From Dr. De Witt's point
of view, one of the crippling features of the seminary's curriculum
was the fact that the entire field of biblical language and exegesis,
Old and New Testament alike, was entrusted to a single professor.
For twenty-one years De Witt had tried to teach such a vast
field, so he knew firsthand the problems which it involved.

In 1882, in response to a complaint from Professor De Witt,
the synod, acknowledging that other seminaries which were at-
tracting Reformed Church students had biblical departments of
two or three, stated that it was in favor of dividing the biblical
chair when finances would permit. As a temporary measure, the
synod resolved to invite Dr. Chambers to come from New York
and deliver a series on lectures on New Testament exegesis. Char-
acteristically, no provision was made for implementing the invitation financially, and the Chambers lectureship never took place.

The letter which Dr. De Witt sent to the synod in 1883 was
sent to a synod fully aware that it was to receive $50,000 from
the Sage estate for a new professorship. The professor therefore
called upon the synod to supply the seminary's greatest need—

split the biblical chair and use the Sage money to establish a new chair of either Old or New Testament studies.

Synod did not immediately respond to Dr. De Witt's plea. It promised to bear his suggestion in mind, but said it could do nothing until the Sage bequest was actually in hand. It did make a partial concession, however, by authorizing part-time instruction in both Greek and Hebrew, the cost to be paid from the income on the Sage estate. Drs. Chambers and Corwin were secured for the purpose and each eventually received $550 for his work.

It was the synod of 1884 which finally had the Sage estate in hand and as a kind of hundredth birthday present to the seminary decided to make two chairs out of what had been the single chair of biblical literature. Dr. De Witt was given his choice, and much to everyone's surprise he chose the New Testament chair. Since most of his studies had been in Old Testament, everyone wondered why. The answer came on the eighth ballot when John Gulian Lansing, minister of the North Church in West Troy, New York, was chosen the first Gardner Sage Professor of Old Testament Language and Exegesis.

Only thirty-three years old at the time of his election, Dr. Lansing (as he came to be in just a year) was a remarkable person. Born in Damascus to missionary parents, a graduate of Union College, he spent several years as a teacher in Egypt, returning to this country for seminary training. Because of his proficiency in the original languages, he was admitted as a member of the senior class in New Brunswick in 1876, spending only one year there before graduating in 1877.

One can only surmise that during his year at New Brunswick Lansing became a favorite of Dr. De Witt's and that De Witt, as his former mentor, guided his nomination through the eight ballots at General Synod, even to the point of giving up the Old Testament chair in favor of his young friend. Though Dr. Lansing's career at New Brunswick was to be a brief one, it was one which was to leave a lasting stamp on the future of the seminary.

As early as 1882 the synod appointed a special committee to

John Gulian Lansing

plan for the celebration of the centennial of the seminary in 1884. Committees were appointed in each of the three particular synods, together with a central committee of three persons. The overall chairman named was Dr. Paul Van Cleef, pastor of the Second Church in Jersey City. The committee presented the synod the following year with its recommendation that the centennial be observed in October of 1884, with final plans to be approved by synod the following June.

The celebration was held on October 28 and 29, 1884, in both the First and Second Reformed churches in New Brunswick. The opening event was held at 3:00 on Tuesday, October 28, in First Church. After opening devotions conducted by the president of General Synod, Dr. Woodbridge, the senior professor, gave an address entitled "Historical Theology." At an evening session held in First Church, the principal speaker was Dr. Demarest, who presented a history of the seminary.

Wednesday morning's event was held in Second Church with three principal speakers, Dr. Campbell, who spoke on the relation of the college and the seminary; Dr. William Taylor of Newark, whose topic was the influence of the seminary on the denomination; and Dr. Cornelius Crispell, former professor of theology at Hope College, who spoke on the history of theological education in the West.

After lunch, sessions resumed at 2:30 in First Church. Letters of congratulation from the theological faculties of Utrecht, Amsterdam, and Kampen, as well as from a number of American seminaries, were read. Congratulations were brought in person from Princeton Seminary, Hartford Seminary, the Baptist Seminary of Rochester, Lancaster Seminary, Auburn Seminary, Bloomfield Seminary, Drew Seminary, Union Seminary, and Yale Divinity School. There were also special salutations from Rutgers College.

The evening session, the final one in the celebration, was also held in First Church. Dr. Mancius H. Hutton, pastor of Second Church in New Brunswick, outlined plans for future endowments. The principal address was given by Dr. Francis Zabriskie, until recently editor of the Reformed Church's magazine, *The Christian Intelligencer.* Representing the alumni association, Dr. Zabriskie spoke on "The Ministry of the Past and the Future." Some closing remarks by the chairman brought the festivities to an end. The record says that all of the events in the celebration were well attended. The closing program on Wednesday night was held during a severe thunderstorm but the attendance was very large in spite of it.[9]

Though not directly part of the New Brunswick celebration, mention was frequently made of the happy fact that theological education in Holland, Michigan, which had been suspended since 1877, had been resumed in the fall of 1884. At the same time as the mother institution was celebrating its 100th birthday, a new daughter was beginning a long and useful career in the West.

As a charter for the next century, the General Synod of 1884 adopted a new curricular plan for the seminary. It was intended not so much to introduce new subjects as to classify and arrange those which were covered already. The synod saw the curriculum as fitting into four departments. The Department of Exegetical Theology would most likely have two members, since "all high class Seminaries now have one man for Hebrew and another for Greek." (Professor Lansing had not yet been elected when the committee drafted its report.) This department would contain studies in Hebrew and Greek, as well as exegesis, and cover such additional subjects as textual and historical criticism, paleography, and hermeneutics.

The Department of Historic Theology would include the Kingdom of God under both Old and New Covenants, as well as the history of Christian cultus, doctrine, and literature. The Department of Doctrinal Theology covered an outline of the system, the standards of the church, apologetics, and ethics. The Department of Practical Theology included homiletics, catechetics, liturgics, administration, pastoral calling, and evangelism.

The committee also recommended that visiting lecturers be used wherever possible and that instruction in speech as well as personal hygiene ought to be included as part of the curriculum. As a parting shot, it suggested that study be made of extending the seminary course to four years instead of three.[10]

With such a charter the seminary entered its second century. What is remarkable about the 1884 proposal is the way in which it has regulated seminary studies right down to the present time.

VII

Moving Into a New Century

Speaking to a German audience in Berlin in 1854, Dr. Philip Schaff, the Swiss-born and German-educated professor at the German Reformed Seminary in Mercersburg, Pennsylvania, said that in America the finest seminaries possessed impressive buildings, had fine libraries, and were staffed with full-time faculties of four or five professors. In an article, written in 1859, Dr. Schaff specified the schools which he thought were among the most respectable seminaries in the country. Those which he listed in the northeastern part of the United States included Princeton and Pittsburgh, Union and Auburn, Andover, General, and New Brunswick.

Actually Dr. Schaff was being kind; New Brunswick did not at that time have a fourth faculty member, though it was working hard to raise the money to get one. The fact that New Brunswick was included in the list drawn up by a fairly competent observer, however, indicates the image which it wished to project. Even though it represented a much smaller constituency than its sister institutions, it wanted to be considered in the same bracket as its Congregational, Presbyterian, and Episcopal colleagues.

A visitor to the New Brunswick campus at the time of the centennial celebration in 1884 would have come away with an excellent impression. Occupying an entire block along Seminary Place, the school counted seven buildings, including the elegant new house which had just been built for the Suydam professor. The new library contained approximately 35,000 volumes, which made it the equal of most theological libraries in the country. At least one member of the faculty, Dr. De Witt, enjoyed a wide reputation in the field of biblical studies, while his four colleagues were all viewed as knowledgeable and competent teachers.

Thirty-eight students had been enrolled in 1884, a total which in a denomination that numbered only about 82,000 was not bad. Those who were able to see behind the more visible signs of the school's prosperity would have noted that faculty salaries were below average and that only a smaller part of the institution's fairly generous endowment was designated for salaries; by far the larger amount went for building maintenance. But these were problems that could be corrected. By and large, New Brunswick Seminary began its second century convinced that it was one of the major schools of theological learning in the United States.

In spite of all the satisfaction with what had been accomplished in 100 years, there are traces of some uneasiness about the place of the seminary in the life of the church. One of the major addresses given at the centennial celebration was that by Dr. William J. R. Taylor, himself a New Brunswick graduate and pastor of the Clinton Avenue Reformed Church in Newark, New Jersey. Dr. Taylor's address was entitled, "The Influence of the Theological Seminary on the Denominational Life of the Church." At one point Dr. Taylor seemed almost apologetic.

> The Seminary has provided a perennial supply of well-trained and godly ministers to the Church. They have loved the truth and defended it with power and success . . . If it has not had the prestige of large numbers, it has graduated hundreds of accomplished and faithful captains of the Lord's host who have never turned their backs to the enemy. If it has not been conspicuous for its contributions to Theological Science and Literature in former times, it has furnished within the present score of years, some Biblical exegetes. Critics, translators and revisers of our English Bible who rank with the foremost of their class. While its alumni fill its own chairs with honor to themselves and to the Institution, it has given two of its choicest and best to a sister Seminary . . .[1]

Dr. Taylor is certainly referring to Dr. De Witt, the one bright light in an otherwise rather pedestrian New Brunswick faculty, and possibly to Dr. John Lillie, a Scotsman who had graduated from the seminary in 1835 and was the author (or translator) of several New Testament commentaries. The two alumni who, as Dr. Taylor pointed out in a footnote, were at Hartford Seminary were Dr. Chester Hartranft (who became its president in 1888) and Dr. Matthew Riddle, one of the first American professors to have studied in Germany, who left Hartford in 1887 to become a faculty member and ultimately the president of what is today Pittsburgh Seminary.

What Dr. Taylor did not mention was the fact that the major pulpits of the denomination were not calling New Brunswick graduates. In 1884, for example, of the eleven major Reformed churches in the metropolitan area, only two were filled with graduates of the seminary. Of the four ministers of the Collegiate Church in New York, Dr. Chambers had studied at New Brunswick for one year, but graduated from Princeton; the other three were all graduates of other seminaries. The Reformed Church had a number of large congregations in rural areas or in county towns which were almost all filled with New Brunswick graduates. But the major pulpits in places like New York, Brooklyn, Albany, Newark, and Philadelphia were almost entirely occupied by graduates of Princeton, Union, Andover, or, in an increasing number of instances, by Canadians or Scotsmen.

Evidently pulpit committees from these metropolitan churches must have been aware of some lack in New Brunswick graduates which today it is impossible to identify. One can only hazard a guess that part of the problem was the very conservative stance which the seminary had chosen to take. Reading all the addresses offered at the centennial, one is impressed by the repeated emphasis on the seminary's theological conservatism. Most often it is praised; occasionally, as in the case of the delegate from Union Seminary, it is mildly chided.

Perhaps you are a little more conservative and emphatic in your Calvinism than we are. Possibly we are a little more progressive than you are . . . But you and we, I am sure, are of the same mind in this, that the framers of our admirable Confessions and Catechisms

were not infallible or inspired men . . . Nor do we disagree in this,
that since those faithful men lived more than two and a half or three
centuries ago, a great deal of light has broken forth out of God's Holy
word.[2]

What was considered a lack of openness to all kinds of new
currents might do very well in a country village or a small county
town, but it hardly met the needs of metropolitan areas where
the survival of a congregation often depended on its ability to
attract former Congregationalists and Presbyterians.

In one thing, however, New Brunswick graduates had excelled
as Dr. Taylor did not hesitate to point out.

It gave our first American Missionary to China in the person of
David Abeel—leader of a noble band; its sons were among the first
and foremost to take the gospel to Japan; and India has no more
effective Christian laborers than those of the Arcot mission.[3]

There was no way he could have known at the time he spoke that
young Professor Lansing who had but recently joined the faculty
would be responsible for still another missionary first by persuading some of his students to invade Arabia in the name of
Christ!

It is somewhat indicative of the prevailing mood at New Brunswick that its first endowed lectureship, given in 1873 by Nicholas
Vedder of Utica, New York, was on "The Present Aspects of Modern Infidelity, Including its Cause and Cure." Even though the
railroad bonds which Mr. Vedder had given as an endowment
failed to pay interest after 1875, the lectures continued to be
given until 1889 on such topics as "The Science of Divine Truth
Impregnable," "The Truths and Untruths of Evolution," "Nega-
tions of Infidelity," and "Inspiration, Literal and Direct."

The seminary began its second century with a faculty of five:
Dr. Woodbridge who had occupied the chair of church history
for twenty-seven years; Dr. De Witt who had taught biblical
literature for twenty-one years but was now free to limit himself

to New Testament studies; Dr. Demarest who had been teaching
pastoral theology and sacred rhetoric for nineteen years; Dr.
Mabon who had been in James Suydam's chair of theology for
only three years; and Dr. Lansing who had just arrived to teach
in the newly-established Department of Old Testament studies.
The faculty now elected one of its members in rotation to serve
as president of the faculty.

Possibly because it realized what was happening to some of
the graduates in terms of calls, the faculty kept reminding the
board of an acute need for instruction in public speaking. Apparently, whatever Dr. Demarest did in sacred rhetoric was not
sufficient. So strongly did the faculty feel about the subject that
for a time the members put their hands in their own pockets to
secure the services of Professor Peabody, an elocution teacher
from Princeton. After a short time, however, the board secured
an annual gift from the North Church in Newark to cover the
professor's fees and he became a standing member of the New
Brunswick staff.

During the first few years after the centennial, however, the
real problem seems to have been the recruitment of new students. Matters reached a crisis in 1886 when a graduating class
of twelve left only ten students in the seminary with no prospects
of any new students from Rutgers which was then the principal
feeder for seminary enrollment. The General Synod of that year
sounded the alarm.

These facts are distressing, if not appalling. Never in the history
of our venerable Theological Seminary have the streams of supply
been so nearly dried up at their source. At the same time it has never
been so well prepared as now to care for young men who need and
wish for a thorough education for their high calling. With its noble
library, its full corps of professors, its new curriculum of studies and
its local advantages, it ought to command, as it deserves, the affection
and confidence of the churches and of their aspirants for the sacred
office. For many years the cry was for buildings, money, books and
other external necessities. These have been liberally supplied.

Now the louder, deeper, sadder cry is for men, pious, gifted, promising, consecrated young men to fill the vacant halls and rooms. [4]

A pastoral letter was prepared to be read in all the churches,
the members of the Board of Superintendents were charged to
bring the matter to the attention of every classis, and the Board
of Education was given responsibility to do whatever it could to
increase the number of candidates for the ministry. When the
seminary reopened in the fall of 1886, there was an entering class
of eleven, as many students as in the other two classes combined.
Though Rutgers had provided no students, there were three from
Hope College and others representing such eastern colleges as
Union and New York University.

It was also during these years that the seminary began to attract
some students among New Brunswick area ministers seeking a
theological education. One of the graduates in 1886, for example,
was the Rev. Junius C. Ayler, pastor of Mt. Zion A. M. E. Church
in the city. Other local pastors attended for a year or so and were
unable to finish because of pastoral duties, but there were some
who, like Mr. Ayler, were able to complete the course. After the
crisis in 1886, enrollments began slowly to rise and there were
no further problems in this area for some time to come.

During these days of both financial and enrollment problems,
it is pleasant to note that the Society of Inquiry developed a
program which brought outstanding ministers and members of
the laity to the seminary campus for a series of addresses on a
variety of topics. The faculty in no way opposed this student
activity but welcomed it as a helpful supplement to the curriculum. No list of these visiting lecturers seems to have survived,
but the students selected persons who could speak on topics of
interest to them and seldom met with a refusal.

No one could have realized it at the time, but a major influence
in the history of New Brunswick Seminary occurred in the fall
of 1886 when John C. Van Dyke was appointed to succeed the
Rev. Peter Quick as librarian of Gardner Sage Library. A layman
with special training in the fine arts and their history, a field in

which he was to do some teaching at Rutgers, Mr. Van Dyke had
served for several years as assistant librarian. He immediately
went to work on a catalogue for the library's collection of 38,738
books and 7,033 pamphlets, one of the largest collections in the
country. (One sign that a new age was overtaking the seminary
was the authorization in 1887 for the librarian to purchase a type-
writer!) Mr. Van Dyke and Professor Lansing became close friends
and the librarian took a great interest in providing space for the
various objects, including a mummy, which the professor sent
home to New Brunswick after a visit to Egypt.

It was Van Dyke also who conceived the idea of hanging the
portraits of faculty members on the gallery railing of Gardner
Sage. He was able to beg some from members of faculty families;
others he had copied from existing portraits. The idea of a faculty
gallery, which has become such a striking feature of Gardner
Sage Library, was one which was entirely developed by Van Dyke.

As Dr. Taylor had noted in his centennial address, a vital concern with missions had been an abiding interest at New Brunswick since Dr. Livingston's time. It was fitting, therefore, that
the Vedder lectures should have been replaced by the Graves
Lectures in Missions in 1888. The Hon. Nathan F. Graves of
Syracuse, New York, a liberal donor to Hope College as well as
to the seminary, provided a sum of money each year to provide
for five lectures on missions. His gift, which he perpetuated with
an endowment of $10,000 when he died in 1896, must have been
interpreted in the broadest sense, since not only distinguished
missionaries such as John Scudder, Robert E. Speer, and Samuel
Zwemer came to New Brunswick on the Graves Foundation, but
also such well-known Christian leaders as Drs. John Hall, George
Adam Smith, and Alexander Gordon.

Mr. Graves's gift came at an appropriate time. Sometime around
1887 Dr. Lansing had invited a small group of students to his
home (the stone house at the corner of George Street and Seminary Place) to talk and pray about the possibility of Christian
missionary work in Arabia. It had always been his deepest desire
to go as a missionary to the lands of Islam himself, but his de-

teriorating health had always stood in his way. Having designed an "Arabian Mission," which he had conceived as an interdenominational effort, he sought students to volunteer for it, offering instruction in Arabic in his own home.

A number of students showed interest, but two, James Cantine ('89) and Samuel Zwemer ('90) volunteered to make the venture. Cantine remembers it in this way.

> . . . the first definite step in my case came through association with Dr. Lansing—in his classroom and in his home. With his inherited interest . . . and with his burning zeal for the evangelization of Moslems, any active display of missionary interest was sure to be drawn into his orbit. Through his class in the study of Arabic, and later in a little weekly prayer meeting for divine guidance, it was gradually made known to three of us . . . that it was God's will that we should offer ourselves for work in Arabia.[5]

Samuel Zwemer's recollection sets the decision in a broader seminary context.

> The missionary spirit in New Brunswick Theological Seminary during 1888 to 1890 was due to several cooperating causes: the Student Volunteer Movement, and Graves Missionary Lectures, the fact that most of our professors were missionary minded and the Society of Inquiry which discussed missions at its regular meeting. All these worked together so that even around the dinner table there would be hot discussions on home and foreign missions.[6]

The Arabian Mission was founded as an independent work in 1889. Cantine left for Syria and Zwemer joined him there a year later. (Philip Phelps, the third volunteer, was never able to go.) Both men met Professor Lansing in Cairo in the fall of 1890 and from there went to begin their work in southwestern Arabia. The mission was transferred to the Reformed Church Board in 1894.

Two vacancies occurred in the faculty in 1892. The first was occasioned by the resignation of Dr. De Witt, presented to the synod in June of that year. Clearly the most distinguished mem-

ber of the faculty, holding honorary degrees from Columbia and
Lafayette as well as Rutgers, he had now reached his seventy-
first birthday. The sudden death of his wife in 1890 had left him
emotionally distressed and in declining health. One might wonder also whether the fact that he was at work on a book, *What
is Inspiration? A Fresh Study of the Question*, was also partially
responsible for the resignation. The book's central thesis of progressive revelation would today seem very mild, but in many
conservative circles of the time it was viewed as radical. In any
event with De Witt's resignation the seminary lost one of the
ablest and most respected of its faculty.

For De Witt's successor the synod reached out to a relative
newcomer to the Reformed Church scene, the Rev. James F.
Riggs, pastor of the Bergen Point Reformed Church in Bayonne,
New Jersey. A graduate of Princeton College and Union Seminary, Riggs had served for eight years in Bayonne when he was
called to the seminary. It is difficult to say just what qualifications
Mr. Riggs, a competent parish pastor and a pleasant person,
brought to the teaching of New Testament Greek and exegesis at
a seminary. The concept that seminary teaching required special
preparation, an idea which had been pioneered at the Harvard
Divinity School after President Eliot reorganized it in 1879, came
slowly to New Brunswick, which continued to see itself as a
school for training ministers, in which the best qualification for
teaching was a successful pastorate.

The other faculty change in 1892 came with the death of Professor Mabon in November at the age of seventy. No scholarly
theologian, he had been a successful teacher whose help his students had valued. To the chair which he had occupied for eleven
years the synod in 1893 elected John Preston Searle, the popular
pastor of the First Reformed Church in Somerville, New Jersey.
Dr. Searle (Rutgers obliged with a honorary degree in the year
of his election), a third generation minister in the Reformed
Church, was well known and well liked in the denomination and
brought new vigor to the institution.

Even though New Brunswick had silently resisted the growing

trend to make seminaries academic centers as well as professional training schools, there was one aspect of this trend which it was no longer possible to resist. The degree programs in American colleges were largely in imitation of the British system. The bachelor of arts degree was awarded at the end of the college course; three years later, the degree holder was almost automatically awarded the master of arts degree. This practice, common in American education, lasted well into the nineteenth century, the last example being in 1881.

The degree question was never a pressing one therefore for most of the nineteenth century, since most seminary graduates would receive the master of arts from their alma maters. The gradual disappearance of the old system, however, raised the question of offering a second degree at the completion of the theological course. One of the first degrees of "bachelor of divinity" was conferred by Harvard Divinity School in 1870, and Harvard's example was almost universally followed in succeeding years.

The question was under study for a short time at New Brunswick before a decision was reached in 1893 to recommend to the trustees of Rutgers those students who were college graduates and who had done special work in a particular course, for the awarding of the bachelor of divinity degree. Students who were unwilling to undertake the extra work or did not possess a college degree would receive a certificate of attendance or, in the case of Reformed Church students, the traditional professorial certificate. For a school which had founded graduate theological education in North America, though sometimes had forgotten its origins, it seemed an appropriate if somewhat belated decision.

Not only did the bachelor of divinity degree involve extra work but it also meant special examinations at the end of each of the three years for those who had enrolled in it. In the class of 1895, the first class for which the new program became operative, two of nine graduates were recommended to Rutgers for the degree; the following year it was three out of ten; in 1897 it was four out

of fifteen. That percentage of interest remained constant for the
next decade, until the regulations were altered in 1904.

Before the nineteenth century ended, however, the faculty was
to undergo some drastic changes. In 1895 two members of the
faculty were battle-scarred veterans—Drs. Demarest and Woodbridge, with a collective sixty-eight years of service to the seminary between them; two, Riggs and Searle, were relative
newcomers; the fifth, Dr. Lansing, had such precarious health
that he was often absent for months at a time. In the year 1898
three of the five had to be replaced.

The first to withdraw was James Riggs. Six years of teaching
had convinced him that the pastorate was his real métier. Since
he had a call to a flourishing Presbyterian Church in East Orange,
New Jersey, he asked the synod of 1898 to release him from his
professorial duties. Dr. Lansing also submitted his resignation,
but too late in the year for the synod to act on it. Shortly after
the synod of 1898 adjourned, word was received of the death of
the venerable Dr. Demarest on June 21, at the age of seventy-
nine!

Synod faced the challenge of rebuilding the faculty as best it
could. For the vacancy created by the resignation of Professor
Riggs it chose (on the seventeenth ballot!) the Rev. John Hamilton Gillespie, a Scotsman by birth, though a graduate of Rutgers
and New Brunswick, who was professor of Greek at Hope College. His teaching career there seemed to suit him for his new
post at the seminary.

Two vacancies were to be filled by the synod of 1899. After the
hassle of 1898, when it had required seventeen ballots to elect
Dr. Gillespie, synod resolved to try a different method of nomination, especially since there were two vacancies to be filled with
successors for Drs. Demarest and Lansing. Prior nominations
from the classes had been requested with the result that for the
chair of pastoral theology twelve men had been nominated by
twenty-three classes. Two additional names were presented by
classes which had not previously reported. Synod then named

three candidates, but the three had already been named by various classes.

The election went to Dr. Ferdinand Schenck, a graduate of Princeton and New Brunswick, who had the distinction of having served as a practicing attorney for several years between college and seminary. Widely regarded as one of the outstanding preachers of the denomination, Dr. Schenck was serving the University Heights Church in New York at the time of his election.

The same system was followed in electing a successor to Dr. Lansing in Old Testament studies. Nine men were nominated by twenty-three classes, three of whom received the extra endorsement of nomination by General Synod. The candidate elected was John H. Raven, pastor of the Reformed Church in Metuchen, New Jersey, who had already done yeoman service in filling in for Dr. Lansing during the times he was absent because of illness, and was therefore well known to the seminary community. One small fact should be noted in connection with the election of a new Old Testament professor's salary. The salary for all New Brunswick faculty was still $2,500 a year, painfully low for the time. Gardner Sage's endowment, however, did not yield that amount of money annually. Mr. Raven, therefore, was paid the income from the Sage Fund (together with the use of a house) with the promise that his salary would be increased to the level of that of his colleagues as soon as the financial condition of the seminary would permit.

That financial situation had been a concern since 1898 when a special committee reported that falling interest rates had depleted the school's annual income to a dangerous point. Part of the problem was the general assumption in the Reformed Church that the seminary was too well endowed to require any help.

> . . . hitherto for a generation the church—not having been asked for new gifts—has not known of the Seminary's needs: has, on the contrary, been widely under the impression that what it had received so long ago sufficed and would suffice for the future.[7]

In pursuit of a larger endowment to remedy the deficit, the committee, remembering the great success of Dr. Cornell, secured the services of Dr. James Demarest of Brooklyn to act as its agent.

Dr. Demarest decided to seek additional endowments of $250,000 in a campaign that was to be concluded in 1901. In the meantime, smaller gifts were raised for immediate needs such as repairing the heating system in Hertzog Hall and paying assessments for paving and sewerage. One such gift was the sum of $1,200 donated by the alumni association which had been formed at the time of the centennial in 1884 and had been meeting annually in connection with the commencement festivities.

While accepting Dr. Demarest's idea of an increased endowment, the Special Finance Committee was also concerned with securing annual gifts from the congregations, an almost unheard of idea in the financing of New Brunswick Seminary. By 1900 the committee and its agents could report that fifty-seven congregations had responded with total gifts of $7,439 and that Mr. Ralph Voorhees had given $25,000 toward the endowment of the chair of New Testament studies.

Dr. Demarest did not enjoy the same success as Dr. Cornell. He reported in 1901 that the endowment had been increased by over $40,000, including the $25,000 gift of Mr. Voorhees. Another $14,500 was included in two wills being probated, as well as $20,000 in "more or less definite" commitments from future estates. Counting future estates as well as gifts in hand, Demarest had increased the principal of the endowment funds by $75,000, but he had also been responsible for increasing the awareness of the churches to their responsibility for annual giving.

The first year of the twentieth century also saw a further change in the faculty. The veteran Samuel Woodbridge, who had occupied the chair of church history since 1857 and was now eighty-two years old, was persuaded to accept the position of professor emeritus at a stipend of $1,000 per year. His long association with the school (he came about the time Hertzog Hall was opened) had made him a beloved figure in the church, but his teaching was increasingly ineffective, especially in the field of church history in which the last half century had seen radical new developments.

The synod followed the same procedure as in 1899. Seventeen men were nominated by thirty classes, and the synod added three names. After several ballots the Rev. William H. S. Demarest, pastor of the Reformed Church in Catskill, New York, was chosen, receiving 101 votes out of 128. A son of the late Professor David Demarest, Dr. Demarest, as he was soon to be, was steeped in New Brunswick tradition. His father had joined the seminary faculty when William was only two and he had grown up on Holy Hill, graduating from both Rutgers and New Brunswick Seminary.[8]

It was with an entirely new faculty that New Brunswick Seminary began the twentieth century. Dr. Searle had the longest term of service and he had not been there ten years. It was also one of the youngest faculties that the seminary had seen in a long time. Dr. Schenck, at fifty-six, was the oldest member of the group; no other member of the faculty had yet reached fifty, while at thirty-one Mr. Raven was not much older than some of his students.

It was a new faculty for a new century. Only the coming years could tell whether it was adequate to carry New Brunswick Seminary into a significant role in meeting the needs of the Reformed Church in the twentieth century.

The faculty c. 1904: John Preston Searle, John Howard Raven,
Samuel Woodbridge, William H. S. Demarest, John Hamilton Gillespie,
Ferdinand Schureman Schenck

VIII

Into the Shadows

The twentieth century began at New Brunswick Seminary with a flurry of activities in several directions. The new faculty, it seemed, was determined to move the school forward. In 1902 Professor Raven applied for what today would be called a sabbatical, the first in the institution's history. He took a year off at his own expense for further study in Europe. This was indeed a startling development. For the traditional New Brunswick mindset, European study was seen as the sure beginning of a loss of faith. At the celebration in 1884, Dr. Taylor had said

> Our whole scheme of doctrine, our history and spiritual life of the Church, are firmly set against every phase of that rationalism which had well nigh emptied the Protestant Churches of Germany and almost driven Calvinism out of Calvin's city and unsettled the foundations of the Mother Church in Holland and made the Heidelberg Catechism as a stranger in the city whose name it bears.[1]

Mercifully, Dr. Taylor went to his grave before a member of the New Brunswick faculty decided to spend a year visiting these same fountainheads of heresy! Professor Raven's decision doubtless resulted not only from a sense of his inadequacy for his task but also from a realization that European training was increasingly essential for a first-class seminary faculty. The pioneer in this direction was the Harvard Divinity School, closely followed by Union Seminary in New York. With a full-time faculty of six, five of whom had studied in Germany, Harvard had set the pattern which other schools gradually began to emulate. As early as 1860, Matthew Riddle, New Brunswick class of 1859, had spent a year in Heidelberg, followed by two more, from 1869 to 1871.

When he returned to America, however, it was to teach at Hartford rather than New Brunswick.

Dr. Abel Huizinga, who had earned a doctorate in Old Testament studies from Johns Hopkins and had previously taught at McCormick Seminary, was asked to fill in for Professor Raven during his sabbatical so that there was no interruption in the curriculum.

In 1900 a question had been raised as to the adequacy of the curriculum in both New Brunswick and Western seminaries, and the faculties of both schools were asked to consider the question. Since no funding was provided, the matter had to be discussed by correspondence until the New Brunswick commencement in May of 1902, when Dr. John W. Beardslee, the president of Western's faculty, was in New Brunswick. He met with the New Brunswick faculty for extended discussion of the questions involved, and he and Dr. Searle, New Brunswick faculty president, presented a joint report to the synod that same year.

Speaking for both faculties, Drs. Beardslee and Searle admitted that in both schools there was need for a "more extended and thorough course in certain directions." The fact was that the curriculum as presently designed confined the course "to what we may call the average intelligence, while some . . . might profitably pursue a more extended course." The addition of a fourth year of study, which some had suggested, was at the present both academically and financially impossible. The solution offered, therefore, was to authorize the schools to establish a post-graduate course of study, limited to such students as were approved for admission.[2]

The same synod of 1902 referred to the seminary faculties a resolution offered by the Committee on Professorate. This resolution forbade any seminary student to marry during his seminary career without the formal consent of the faculty. While exceptions occasionally were made, this resolution became a general policy that was followed for many years to come.

The death of Dr. Carl Meyer on December 4, 1901, had a profound effect on the seminary community. Although never a

member of the faculty, Meyer had a greater influence on many
of the students than did many of the full-time teachers. Meyer,
professor of modern languages at Rutgers from 1869, as well as
pastor of the small German congregation of the Third Reformed
Church, represented the best of German culture and philosophy
which the seminary had so long resisted. A graduate of the University of Halle, he served in Germany as both pastor and teacher
before coming to America in 1862.

Though his task was teaching modern languages at Rutgers,
Dr. Meyer's first love was history, especially the history of the
Reformation. His obituary states that he was also interested "in
the historical development of religion," a subject on which he
had many notes which were "interesting and instructive." One
does not need to read between many lines to understand that
Dr. Meyer represented German historical scholarship as it had
been developing during the nineteenth century.

Add to this the fact that Meyer delighted in meeting with small
groups of students in his home to discuss his favorite topics, and
the picture becomes clear. Especially during Dr. Woodbridge's
declining years as professor of church history, many New Brunswick students gained their real understanding of church history
not from the classroom but from evenings spent with Dr. Meyer.
Dr. Woodbridge taught church history in the traditional chron-
ological way, while Dr. Meyer used the method of historical
development, the chief exponent of which in this country was
then Dr. Philip Schaff of Union Seminary. Meyer's death therefore left a real void in the New Brunswick Seminary community.[3]

Financial achievements at this time seemed to match the new
academic excitement. Although Dr. James Demarest had never
achieved his goal of $250,000 in new endowment of the school,
his success in interesting a sufficient number of congregations to
make an annual contribution to the seminary's budget (the number in 1902 was ninety-three) allowed everyone to breathe a little
more easily. Demarest therefore resigned his position as agent
(development officer) in that same year.

The most creative financial plan was one which had been worked

out by librarian John Van Dyke and the new professor of church
history, Dr. William H. S. Demarest. They launched a plan of
endowing each of the alcoves in Gardner Sage Library at $1,500.
In each alcove a memorial window was to be placed at a cost of
$200; the remaining $1,300 was to go into a special Library Endowment Fund. They felt that a sufficient number of Reformed
Church families could be induced to make this kind of memorial
in a library that already contained more than 45,000 volumes.

To be sure, there were still many physical problems with which
to deal. The city authorities had condemned the boiler in Gardner Sage Library and were demanding its replacement. The new
house which had been built in George Street for the librarian
still had to be paid for. The necessary renovations to Professor
Demarest's house were so extensive after Dr. Woodbridge's forty-
year tenancy that there was no money to pay for them, and the
new professor had to lend the money needed to the board. All
of these things, however, would come in time.

The important thing was that there seemed to be a new confidence in the future of the institution. This confidence was dem-
onstrated through several gifts to the seminary and through some
general improvements. A new bell was placed in the Hertzog
Hall belfry, the gift of Emilie Coles. The widow of James A. H.
Cornell presented a grandfather's clock to the Reading Room (the
clock now adorns the president's house). A generous lady from
Philadelphia donated a Mason and Hamlin organ for the chapel.
The museum was expanded with many articles from the new
Indian mission field in Oklahoma. The sidewalks on the College
Avenue side of the property were replaced through the gifts of
interested friends. An anonymous donor gave $5,000 to create
the Archibald Laidlie publication fund. From the fund's first in-
come the inaugural addresses of Professors Demarest, Raven, and
Schenck were printed, as well as a guide to Gardner Sage Li-
brary, written by John Van Dyke.

The same buoyant spirit continued for the next several years.
Van Dyke's and Demarest's plan for endowed alcoves in the library did very well. By 1904 ten alcoves had been taken and

several of the memorial windows had been installed. Each member of the faculty had established his requirements for post-graduate study, and at least one student had enrolled in the new program. The requirements were that post-graduate students major in a particular department and take a minor study in another. After some experimentation, the faculty decided that after 1904 it would be necessary for students to take a year of post-graduate study in order to receive the bachelor of divinity degree. The Rutgers trustees gave their consent to this decision.

The year 1904 also saw a gift of $12,000 to the seminary endowment from Miss Alida Van Schaick of New York. Since Miss Van Schaick's will provided that the proceeds of her estate should be used for "a scholarship or scholarships" at the seminary, the board decided to designate them for students in the post-graduate program. The physical appearance of the seminary grounds had also taken a vast turn for the better.

> We are glad that the great possibilities of beautifying this finely located piece of ground have appealed to one whose taste and energy and liberality have already made their impress upon every part of Synod's property here. Trees, shrubs, vines, flowers, an arbor here and a rookery there, and graveled paths, provided without the least cost to the (Seminary) Committee, have transformed the north Campus into a thing of beauty.[4]

The anonymous angel referred to in this somewhat glowing account of the seminary campus was Mr. John Bussing, a wealthy layman from New York and the son-in-law of Abraham Van Nest, who had proved such a stalwart friend to the seminary in an earlier time. As a member of General Synod's Committee on Seminary Grounds and Property, Mr. Bussing quietly provided for all kinds of needs on Holy Hill. A good friend of Professor Demarest (there had been long relationships between the Demarest and the Van Nest families), John Bussing proved in many small ways to be a latter-day James Suydam.

The only cloud across the sunny horizon of these days was a

declining student enrollment in both Reformed Church seminaries. In 1904 New Brunswick reported only twenty-six students, while Western enrolled sixteen. By this time, however, the authorities recognized that student enrollments were something subject to periodic fluctuations for which there was no real explanation. Attention was called to the fact but it did not seem to create the panic this time that it had created earlier.

It appears that the reason for this sudden upturn in the seminary's fortunes, apart from the stimulus provided by the dawning of the twentieth century, might have been the new professor of church history. Whatever may have been his abilities as a teacher, he brought new ideas and new energies which the old school needed badly. This was recognized in the report of the committee to the synod of 1904.

> The committee wish to acknowledge the fact that under a kind Providence the substantial gains in our work during the past year and the encouraging report we are subsequently able to make are largely due to the tact and energy of Prof. W. H. S. Demarest which, without seeking release from an hour of Seminary work and without compensation, he has placed most effectively at our service.[5]

Since so much of the seminary's energetic reorganization to meet the needs of the twentieth century had come from the creative activity of Dr. Demarest, it must have come as a shock, though probably as no surprise, to learn in 1905 that the trustees of Rutgers College had chosen him to serve as acting president and then in 1906 elected him president. Dr. McCormick's description of Dr. Demarest's vision for Rutgers College could well describe what he had done for New Brunswick Seminary during his short time there.

> With his strong ties to the old College, to the Dutch Church, and to traditional values, Dr. Demarest was not disposed to equate changes with progress or to embrace the fad of the moment. Yet in an eminently practical manner he recognized that the College must be "lib-

eral in adjustment to the life and exigencies of the times while not
swayed by every wind of educational doctrine." Even stronger than
his loyalty to the past was his desire to enhance the stature of Rutgers,
and to accomplish that objective he was prepared to be tolerant of
innovations.[6]

Just about the time that Dr. Demarest was chosen acting president of Rutgers (while still retaining his seminary chair), both
New Brunswick and Western seminaries received an unexpected
bonanza from the Reformed Church Board of Education. That
body discovered that it had a sizeable amount of unexpended
income in its scholarship funds and, on advice of counsel, offered
to give each seminary $1,000 per year for some special project,
so long as the unexpended surplus lasted.

The New Brunswick faculty did not hesitate to accept such an
offer. With money in hand, it invited Dr. J. Frederic Berg, then
pastor of the Reformed Church at Port Richmond on Staten Island, to become lector in "sacred history and biblical theology."
It seems evident that what he was asked to do was to teach
courses in English Bible. This new position was created in recognition of several facts. A growing number of students were
obtaining dispensations from the original languages, especially
Hebrew, and a growing number of students coming to the seminary were from denominations that did not require these languages for ordination. In addition, there were some students
whose biblical background from their college training was so
spotty that they needed some basic courses in biblical history.

In any event, the arrangement begun with Dr. Berg lasted
until his election as a full professor in 1911. A good scholar and
a fine teacher, he was the first member of the New Brunswick
faculty since Dr. Livingston to have an earned doctorate, which
he had obtained in Old Testament studies from Columbia in 1896.
In welcoming him to New Brunswick, the board expressed the
hope that his lectorship would soon develop into a sixth full-time
faculty position. It should be noted that while he served as lector,
Dr. Berg continued as pastor of his congregation in Staten Island.

The resignation of Dr. Demarest confronted the General Synod of 1906 with the need to elect a new professor of church history. Once again, nominations were by classes, a procedure which produced nine candidates. After seven ballots, the appointment went to Dr. Edward P. Johnson, pastor of the First Church in Albany, New York. Dr. Johnson was of Presbyterian background and had served the Albany congregation since 1891. He had been active in denominational affairs, having been elected president of General Synod in 1900, and was well known throughout the Reformed Church. His qualifications for teaching church history, however, were minimal. Johnson's real interests and teaching skills were in the areas of hymnology and worship. All in all, it was not a happy appointment for New Brunswick or for the new professor.

It was at the time of Dr. Johnson's election that the General Synod appointed a committee to devise a better system of choosing seminary faculty than the classical nomination and synodical election method currently in use. That system consumed enormous amounts of time with numerous ballots and put an unfair burden on synodical delegates who knew little about the candidates or the qualifications needed for the job. The result was that they tended to vote for the name they knew best, as probably had happened in the case of Dr. Johnson.

The committee reported in 1907 that a nomination for the professorate ought to be the responsibility of the Board of Superintendents of each seminary. If two-thirds of the synod concurred in the nomination, it would be official, although up to three further nominations could be made from the floor. Synod concurred with the recommendation, and by 1908 it was part of the Reformed Church *Constitution*. Dr. Johnson was therefore the last New Brunswick professor elected under the old system.

The year 1906 was a memorable one also because it was in that year that the city of New Brunswick decided at last to macadamize Seminary Place. Up to that time it had been what someone once described as "a sometime street and sometime sea of red mud." The new pavement, for which the seminary had to bear part of the cost, added greatly to the tidiness of the seminary campus, which under Mr. Bussing's devoted care was taking on an increasingly handsome appearance.

For the remaining years of the decade the seminary carried on in a pretty even fashion with its full-time faculty of five and a half, regularly supplemented by lectures in missions, music, and elocution, together with the visitors who came to the campus at the invitation of the Society of Inquiry. While boilers and plumbing seemed to be perpetual problems, the real question was the future of Gardner Sage Library. Originally designed to hold 40,000 volumes, it had now reached a catalogue of 50,000, with the result that books were double stacked on the shelves, moved to the basement, or stacked in alcoves. Lienau's original design for the building had called for two transepts, neither of which had ever been built. Nearly every report from this era on called for some generous donor to step forward with $25,000 to build one of the transepts to relieve the crowding situation. The generous donor never appeared, but the committee, in hope, kept asking.

Beneath the placid surface at the seminary, there were rumblings of discontent. Several members of the class of 1912 had taken their first year of seminary at Princeton in protest against

Panorama of Holy Hill

what they believed to be a stagnant and ineffective faculty at New Brunswick. That stirred up some of the New Brunswick students to express their own discontent. Berg and Gillespie were both considered effective teachers, but that was where it ended.

Searle and Schenck had both been with the institution for many years and were doing the same old things in the same old ways. It was already clear that Johnson had been a mistake. While Raven was a competent teacher, he acted as though Hebrew were the only subject in the curriculum, making unreasonable demands on student time. Why should students travel to New Brunswick, especially from distant Michigan, when a more stimulating experience was available at Princeton?

As is so often the case, the only member of the faculty to be responsive to such complaints was one whom the students universally respected. Dr. Gillespie submitted his resignation to the synod of 1911, alleging reasons of health, though everyone knew what the real reasons were. With his sensitive nature, he felt that the student complaints were aimed at him and nothing could change his mind at that point.[7]

Dr. Gillespie's successor, chosen by the synod of 1911 under the new rules, was the popular Dr. Berg, the new professor of Hellenistic Greek and exegesis, even though his training had been in the Old Testament field. To remedy the situation, the board asked Dr. Gillespie to remain as instructor in textual criticism and missions, a position which he accepted at a part-time stipend of $1,000 per year.

Since coming to New Brunswick Seminary in 1899, Dr. Raven had been housed in the Cook House, at the corner of Seminary Place and George Street, which Sage and Suydam had purchased for the school some years before. A factory (Johnson and Johnson), which "ran by night as well by day," had now moved in across the street, and Professor Raven decided to vacate the premises and purchase his own dwelling. The seminary authorities were at first afraid to dispose of the property for fear of further industrialization of the neighborhood, but their old friend at Rutgers, President Demarest, purchased the house for the college for $11,000 and accepted a restrictive deed prohibiting any commercial use of the lot or house. (Could he somehow have sensed that this might be the home in which he would spend his retirement years?) The $11,000 from the sale of the house was invested against the day when it might be needed to provide a home for a sixth professor. Some lots had already been purchased in Bishop Place with that in mind.

The year 1911 also marked the centennial of the Society of Inquiry. A history of the society, written by Luman Shafer of the class of 1912 (later to be the distinguished secretary of the Board of Foreign Missions), was published, as well as an alumni directory, which had been prepared by Dr. Raven.

The big news of the time was the totally unexpected Carver estate, the exact amount of which was unknown. Several times during its settlement the board had to request churches to continue their giving and not stop because of this unexpected windfall. The story is a somewhat romantic one. During his work of improving the appearance of grounds and buildings, Mr. Bussing had placed a bronze tablet in the entrance of Hertzog Hall, commemorating the donor, Mrs. Ann Hertzog. (The tablet is now on the wall in Hertzog Dining Hall.) A Philadelphia lady paid a casual visit to the seminary in the early years of the twentieth century, and when she saw the tablet, she introduced herself as Mrs. Ann Carver, a niece of the late Mrs. Hertzog.

When Mrs. Carver died in 1911, her will contained a bequest of $25,000 for Gardner Sage Library, a bequest which apparently her aunt had requested her to make. A codicil to the will left her home at 15th and Arch streets in Philadelphia to the seminary in a largely unrestricted way. No one knew the value of the real estate, but since it was in central Philadelphia, it was thought to be considerable. Actually, for a New Jersey school whose directors were a New York corporation to sell a piece of property in Pennsylvania proved to be quite a legal hassle, and it was several years before the transaction could be completed. When the Carver estate was finally settled, $72,750 was realized from the property, house, lot, and stable. While the amount was not as large as had been rumored, it was a tidy addition to the seminary's endowment and whetted the appetite of those who were planning for a sixth full professor.

After the flare-up of 1911 the seminary faculty decided to modernize both its curriculum and its nomenclature, and a number of changes were adopted in 1913. Some of the changes were merely cosmetic, as, for example, the change from the chair of didactic and polemic theology to the chair of systematic theology. Others were more substantial. Some additional subjects were added to both the Old and New Testament departments and the special lectorship, which was to become the sixth professorship, was to be in biblical theology and the English Bible. Furthermore, the time of instruction was increased from fourteen to sixteen hours per week. Finally, all students not taking Hebrew or Greek were to be required to take equivalent work in the exegesis of the English Bible with Dr. Gillespie.

The modern world finally caught up with the campus of New Brunswick Seminary in 1913. Gardner Sage Library was wired for electricity! Up to this point the building had had no artificial illumination and had had to close every day at sundown. Electricity was also placed in the chapel and Society of Inquiry room in Hertzog Hall. A stereopticon machine was purchased for the Society of Inquiry room, the beginning of audio-visual education at New Brunswick Seminary. Professor Berg's home (now the president's house) was wired for electricity the following year and the other faculty homes were done in turn.

Another student flare-up occurred in 1915, this time over Hebrew. The General Synod received a petition from the New Brunswick student body asking that Hebrew be made an elective during the middler and senior years. The petitioners felt that the introduction to Hebrew given in the junior year was sufficient. The petition was accompanied by a response from the faculty urging that Hebrew be retained for the full three years in order to meet the requirements of classical examinations and to obviate hiring a full-time faculty member to teach the Old Testament in English. As was to be expected, the General Synod politely refused to grant the petition, but did urge the faculty to reduce the number of hours of Hebrew study in the middler and senior years.

In 1917 Dr. Berg accepted a call to the Flatbush Dutch Church in Brooklyn, New York. It is impossible to say for what reasons he decided to leave the seminary where he was clearly one of the most popular members of the faculty. There are indications, however, that he had grown restless in an institution where everything worked in a set pattern and where all the answers were presumed to be available.[8] To fill the vacancy created by his resignation, the synod of 1917 elected the Rev. Dr. John W. Beardslee, Jr., professor of New Testament at Western Seminary, and the second New Brunswick faculty member to have an earned doctorate. Dr. Beardslee's coming to New Brunswick in 1917 began a career which was to bring much luster to the institution.

Another change in procedure, though a minor one, also occurred in 1917. In prior years, commencement exercises had been held in the evening in either the First or Second Reformed churches in New Brunswick. Commencement of 1917 was held in the late forenoon in Kirkpatrick Chapel on the campus of Rutgers, thus beginning a tradition which has continued to this day.

In 1918, looking toward the creation of a new faculty position in English Bible and Christian education, the board secured the services of two men—the Rev. Simon Blocker of Paterson, New Jersey, as lector in biblical theology, and the Rev. Dr. John Beardslee, who had recently retired after a distinguished career at Western Seminary and had now come to New Brunswick to make his home with his son.

By this time the United States was fully involved in the First World War, which had a far more drastic effect on the seminary than did the Civil War. Numbers of students left the seminary to enter the service, thereby depleting already reduced ranks. Fuel shortages required the closing of Gardner Sage Library evenings for the winter months of January through March and the total closing of Suydam Hall during the same period. One won-

ders whether the jubilant celebrants of the Armistice in 1918 had
any idea of the strange new world which they were entering.

The post-war era began well for the seminary. In addition to
lectors Beardslee and Blocker, numerous visiting lecturers came
to the seminary to supplement the instruction offered there. In
1918, the alumni association sponsored two series of lectures, one
on the country church and one on the city church, given by well-
known American leaders. A missionary conference became an
annual event on the seminary campus. In 1919 Edward P. St.
John from the YMCA Training School in New York was hired to
teach a semester's course in Christian education. Faculty salaries,
long pitifully inadequate, in 1919 were raised to $3,000 a year
because anything less than that was not worthy of "the dignity
and importance of a Theological Professor."

One of the most significant developments of the war years was
a conference held in the summer of 1918 in Cambridge, Massachusetts, sponsored by Harvard University. Forty-nine American
and Canadian seminaries sent delegates. New Brunswick was represented by Professors Johnson and Schenck. The purpose of the
conference was to consider the future of theological education in
North America in the post-war age. From this conference there
came a Continuation Committee, of which Dr. Searle was a member. This committee led to the formation of the Association of
Theological Schools, of which New Brunswick has been a member since the beginning.

The post-war years did, however, in some subtle and some not
so subtle ways, take their toll on the seminary. Post-war inflation
meant that the cost of maintaining buildings and paying salaries
rose rapidly, straining the means of the school to the utmost.
Faculty salaries which only recently had been raised to $3,000
had to go to $3,500, and the end was not in sight. The cost of
fuel and electricity jumped alarmingly, but the interest rates on
the endowment did not rise accordingly. The economic prospect
was bleak indeed.

The more subtle result of the post-war era was a marked de-
crease in enrollment. Student bodies which a few years ago had
averaged thirty-five to forty now numbered twenty to twenty-

five. In spite of several successful Life Work Conferences held at the seminary by the Society of Inquiry for high school and college students, entering classes were smaller each year. Obviously the rapid secularization of the time had radically depleted the number of those considering the ministry as a career.

The situation at New Brunswick was worsened by the death of the senior Dr. Beardslee in 1921 and notice from both Dr. Gillespie and Mr. St. John that they would be terminating their lectureships in 1923. If ever the sixth professor was needed, it was now, but the high cost of living had pretty well used up the income that had been set aside for him.

Morale was further weakened when Dr. Searle had a stroke (which ultimately proved to be fatal) in April of 1922. As president of the faculty, he had been the driving center for most of the seminary's accomplishments and had been a tireless worker on its behalf. There seemed to be no one else on the faculty with the same administrative abilities who could take his place.

Because Western Seminary had been facing some of the same problems, the General Synod of 1922 adopted the following resolution.

> While we congratulate both Seminaries upon what they have accomplished with the means at their disposal, we must recognize squarely . . . that both are badly hampered by lack of teachers and equipment. The maintaining of two theological seminaries by a denomination no larger than ours is no easy matter . . . The recent enormous increase in the cost of maintaining any ecclesiastical institution . . . forces us to consider the future of our two seminaries more thoughtfully and anxiously than ever before . . .
>
> We recommend, therefore, that the President of General Synod be instructed to appoint a committee of not less than three men, ministers or layman, who shall consider the condition of our Seminaries and report to the next General Synod.[9]

The committee appointed consisted of three ministers—Henry Veldman, Addison Jones, and Anthony Luidens—and one elder—John Trompen. On their recommendations rested the future of New Brunswick Seminary and the form it should take.

IX

The Demarest Decade: A Second Spring

Once it had become common knowledge that a special committee had been appointed to study the future of the two seminaries in the Reformed Church, the pages of *The Christian Intelligencer*, the denominational magazine, were frequently filled by ministers who had suggestions to offer. In the issue of November 1, 1922, Dr. Frederic Berg, pastor of the Flatbush Church in Brooklyn, suggested that the future of New Brunswick Seminary lay in establishing closer relationships with Rutgers, since many of the courses needed for an enlarged curriculum were already being taught there. The issue of February 21, 1923, contained a thoughtful article by Dr. William Bancroft Hill, a highly-respected leader in the Reformed Church and a member of the Vassar faculty. Dr. Hill's suggestion was that since the elimination of either school was unthinkable, the best solution was to make use of both but in a cooperative way.

According to the plan which Dr. Hill outlined, a student should be required to spend his first two years at one school, and his third, plus a post-graduate year, at the other. Such a plan would give the seminaries a faculty of ten, just about the same number as Princeton or Union. He went on to point out that it was the lack of depth in the faculties which accounted for the fact that six recent graduates of Hope College and three from Rutgers were students at Princeton, while two other Rutgers graduates were at Union. Though nothing came of Dr. Hill's plan at the time, it was a remarkable prophecy of the program which was to be adopted more than forty years later.

The two most critical articles were written by the Rev. Lawrence French, a recent New Brunswick alumnus who was doing graduate study at Rutgers, and the Rev. W. Louis Sahler, an

132

older alumnus who at the time was pastor in Harlingen, New Jersey. Mr. French asserted that in a short time the future of New Brunswick would no longer be a debatable question since there would be no students. Unless the seminary altered its curriculum to include practical social and church experience, he saw no future for it. Mr. Sahler went even further. The cheapest solution to the problem, he wrote, was to close the school and subsidize any student who did not wish to attend Western to attend Princeton as a substitute.

After much of this kind of discussion, the report which the special committee presented to the synod in 1923 may have seemed like something of an anti-climax. The report was a thorough study comprising almost seventeen closely-printed pages in the minutes of General Synod.[1] The committee first examined the various alternatives which had appeared in the *Intelligencer* and gave its reasons for rejecting all of them. Accepting the fact that two seminaries were a necessity in the Reformed Church in America, the report then suggested a totally new plan of organization for both schools, though the reorganization was more drastic for New Brunswick where the problems were more severe.

The plan for New Brunswick recommended the appointment of a president who would be responsible not only for the internal management of the school but also for representing it in the Reformed Church and ecumenically as well. In place of the three groups—superintendents, Committee on Property, Committee on Finance—which had been operating the school, often with overlapping jurisdictions, the committee proposed two: the superintendents who would be responsible for the spiritual and theological well-being of the school and a Board of Managers to be composed of six ministers and six laymen, together with the president of the board. Virtually every aspect of the operation of the institution, including proposals for faculty appointments, was to be the responsibility of the managers who were to meet at least three times a year.

The plan was apparently approved by the General Synod with very little debate. One of the reasons for the ease of its passage

may well have been the seminary's nomination for a new professor of theology. Dr. Searle had never recovered from his stroke,
and a second stroke had been responsible for his death in the
summer of 1922. The nomination of Edward Strong Worcester
of Bellows Falls, Vermont, to be his successor resulted in one of
the most bruising battles in the history of either General Synod
or New Brunswick Seminary.

Who was Edward Strong Worcester? The son of a Presbyterian
pastor who briefly served as professor of theology at Union Seminary, Dr. Worcester was a graduate of Princeton University and
Hartford Seminary who had done graduate study in Berlin. After
serving pastorates in Congregational churches in Norwich, Con-
necticut, and Madison, Wisconsin, he had become minister of
the First Congregational Church in Bellows Falls, Vermont, in
1922.

What had led New Brunswick Seminary to select Dr. Worcester for its vacancy? Here the reports vary and a good deal of
speculation is possible. The written record states that New Brunswick's attention had been drawn to him by Professor Waldo Pratt
of the Hartford faculty and that his suggestion was enthusiastically
seconded by a member of the Rutgers faculty who had at one
time been a member of Dr. Worcester's congregation at Madison.

All of that is doubtless true, but one wonders if more than that
may not lie beneath the surface. After all, a New Brunswick
graduate had been the president of Hartford when Dr. Worcester
was a student there. Is it impossible to imagine that Dr. Hartranft
had at some time said to his old friend and former parishioner,
William H. S. Demarest, "Here is a young man to watch in the
future"? Hartranft's successor as Hartford president had been
Rockwell Harmon Potter, formerly a Reformed Church minister.
Is it again impossible to imagine that the committee may have
turned to him for suggestions? Relations between New Brunswick
and Hartford had been close for many years. In 1924 there were
eight Reformed Church students at Hartford, whimsically known
as the "Dutch Army."

In any event, it was this forty-seven-year-old New England

Congregational minister whose name the superintendents presented to the synod. Of course, the name had been known before the synod met and many persons had been in correspondence with Dr. Worcester to determine the orthodoxy of his Calvinism. His replies satisfied most but not everyone. A group of delegates came to the synod of 1923 determined to block the election in any way possible. Their first chance came in two executive sessions which the synod held on Thursday, June 8, from 9:00 in the morning until mid-afternoon. While no one knows what was said at those sessions, it is easy to surmise that the pros and cons of the Worcester nomination were hotly debated but that its opponents were unable to have the name withdrawn.

When the nomination came to the floor, several other names were suggested, but none could obtain the two-thirds vote necessary to become official. Dr. Worcester was the sole nominee, but under the rules of synod he had to obtain three-fourths of the vote, to be elected. After seven ballots, it was obvious that this was not possible. His opponents, having no other candidate for whom to vote, simply turned in blank ballots to prevent his obtaining the necessary number of votes. Finally, an exhausted synod held a special session at 11:00 p.m. The number of those voting for Dr. Worcester on this eighth ballot had not changed, but whether his opponents had decided to give up the battle or simply had tired and gone to bed, they showed up in significantly smaller numbers so that about midnight the candidate was elected. This time, however, the election was not made unanimous, as was usually the case, because of some conscientious objectors who refused to permit it.

It had been a long, hard fight, and one naturally wonders who had engineered it. Looking over the list of possibilities, there seems to be only one person who had the skill and determination to see it through. It certainly was no one from a demoralized and discouraged faculty. There is only one name on the list of the Board of Superintendents who could have done it, though he may have had some helpful allies. William H. S. Demarest, president of Rutgers, though he had not been with the seminary since

1906, had never lost interest in its welfare and in 1923 was a member of the Board of Superintendents from the Classis of New Brunswick.

Demarest was not a delegate to this synod, which met in Asbury Park, just a short distance from New Brunswick. Probably his Rutgers experience had further sharpened his skills at behind-the-scenes operations and he put them to good use in Asbury Park. Convinced of the need for new blood at New Brunswick Seminary, Demarest had become convinced that Dr. Worcester was the man to bring it, and he used all the pressure of his not inconsiderable influence to achieve this goal.

Future historians may debate whether all of this strategizing was worthwhile. Dr. Worcester served at the seminary until his death in 1937. Highly respected and thoroughly competent, his contribution to the school was not a small one. On the other hand, the fracturing caused by his election took many years to heal. New Brunswick's reputation as a "liberal, modernist" school unworthy of Reformed Church support dates from the Worcester battle. It was certainly the most violent shove into a new pattern that the seminary had ever experienced.

The Survey Committee in 1923 had complained of the weakness of the New Brunswick faculty. The first change occurred with Dr. Worcester's election, but there were two more changes to follow. Dr. Schenck, aware that the special committee had recommended compulsory retirement for faculty members at age seventy, submitted his resignation to the synod in 1924. He was seventy-nine at the time. At the height of his powers, he had been one of the most creative and stimulating members of the faculty with a long list of publications to his credit, but his advancing years and failing eyesight had made him less and less capable for his task.

Dr. Johnson, professor of church history, died suddenly and unexpectedly on May 31, 1924, at the age of seventy-four. In its 1923 report the special committee had said

New Brunswick Seminary is at present not strongly manned. This is a universal conviction. Hence it is the unanimous opinion of your committee that General Synod should charge the Board of Superintendents, in cooperation with the proposed Board of Managers, to consider seriously and *at once* the solution of this problem which more than any other stands in the way of securing a larger student body.[2]

The retirement of Dr. Schenck and the sudden death of Dr. Johnson, of course, meant that necessary faculty changes would occur.

With Dr. Searle's death, Dr. Raven was chosen president of the faculty, and after the adoption of the special report in 1923, he also became acting president of the seminary. This was, of course, a temporary measure since Dr. Raven far preferred teaching to administration. When it became increasingly apparent that Dr. Demarest was no longer happy in his Rutgers presidency, he was approached about assuming the new presidency of New Brunswick.

It is impossible to say just when Demarest accepted the idea. As has been noted in the Worcester affair, he had begun to act more and more like a president after Dr. Searle's death. Many changes which were inaugurated during Dr. Raven's interim presidency were probably the inspiration of Dr. Demarest. In any event, the synod of 1924 elected Demarest president of New Brunswick Seminary, with minor teaching responsibilities, and he assumed his new office on January 1, 1925. A current issue of the *Intelligencer* hailed the new president jubilantly and predicted great things for the future of the seminary.

Dr. Demarest inherited a rather forlorn institution. It had a strong biblical department in the persons of Drs. Beardslee and Raven and an untried theologian in Dr. Worcester. Illness and infirmity meant that the remaining faculty was largely adjuncted. The question of a sixth professorship had been under discussion for some years. The school's $700,000 endowment was no longer adequate for an age of rising costs and falling interest rates. Worst

William H. S. Demarest

of all was the drop in student enrollment. In 1923-4 the total student body numbered thirteen, with a junior class of two members! It almost seemed that the dire predictions of Mr. French were beginning to come true. There was an obvious lack of confidence in the school on the part of the denomination.

Even before Dr. Demarest's assumption of the presidency, some new moves were made to remedy the situation, moves which to this author at least bear the traces of his hand. Ever since the bachelor of divinity degree had been shifted to a postgraduate status in 1904, it had had very few takers, even though the Van Schaick Fund had provided a small scholarship. Obviously, most seminary graduates did not want to spend another year gaining a degree, but were anxious to get on with their calling.

In 1923 a new program was inaugurated with some success. One day each week two courses were offered for ordained clergy. The first curriculum is interesting.

First Semester:
    Philosophy of Religion—Dr. Cantrall (interim theologian)

    Age of the Reformation—Dr. Johnson
    Rural Sociology—Professor Keller of Rutgers
    The Kingdom of God—Dr. Blocker
    The Gospel of Luke—Dr. Beardslee

Second Semester:
    Authority in Religion—Dr. Worcester
    Age of the Reformation—Dr. Johnson
    The Kingdom of God—Dr. Blocker
    The Gospel of Luke—Dr. Beardslee

With few exceptions, each course required two hours. When a student had completed two of them, he was eligible to receive the bachelor of divinity degree through Rutgers. Eighteen students signed up the first year the new program was offered.

The Rev. Theodore F. Bayles, a graduate of Union College and New Brunswick Seminary and one of the first recipients of the bachelor of divinity degree, was chosen professor of practical theology by the synod in 1924. At the time of his election he was pastor of the Reformed Church in Walden, New York. Dr. Johnson's death occurred so close to the time of the synod that no nomination to the chair of church history was possible. Dr. Loetscher of Princeton filled the vacancy, with the help of Dr. Worcester.

The year 1925, the first year of Dr. Demarest's official presidency, saw a large expansion of the post-graduate program. In addition to the offerings in New Brunswick, the same program was held both in Albany and New York, with a total enrollment of forty-two, the largest group being the one in Albany. And this at a time when the total enrollment in the seminary was fourteen! This post-graduate program must have been one of the country's first in continuing theological education and certainly gave the seminary a new lease on life.

The year 1925 also saw the election of a successor to Dr. Johnson in the chair of church history. Milton Hoffman, who was unanimously chosen by the synod that year, had had an unusual educational background. After graduating from Hope College in

1909, he won a Rhodes Scholarship and spent the next three years at Oxford, where he received a second bachelor's degree in church history. Returning to this country in 1912, he entered Western Seminary from which he graduated in 1914 and immediately thereafter became professor of Latin at Hope. In 1917 he became the first Reformed Church president of Central College in Pella, Iowa, from which he was called to the New Brunswick chair.

Dr. Hoffman brought unusual talents to the New Brunswick post. Not only had he had unusual training in the field of church history, but he was the first representative of the Dutch Middle West to teach in the seminary. One cannot help wondering whether his choice was in part dictated by the fact that after the Worcester battle, his appointment was intended to allay western fears that New Brunswick was passing into strange hands. In any event, Dr. Hoffman's historical skills and his sensitivity to social issues provided a rare combination for the seminary.

Dr. Demarest's new faculty team was now complete except for the sixth professorship. Even though he had determined that it should be a chair of Christian education, he was not yet ready with a nominee. In addition to rebuilding the faculty, he had skillfully pried loose some unexpended income for necessary repairs to Hertzog Hall, raised faculty salaries to $3,600 per year, and begun a campaign to raise additional funds from friends of the seminary. Even though he had been president of the seminary for only six months, Dr. Demarest was the subject of jubilant praise from synod's Committee on Professorate.

> Under the leadership of Rev. W. H. S. Demarest, an advance is being made in every department. With vacancies in the faculty filled by able teachers well qualified for their respective departments, with an enlarged program for carrying on graduate instruction in various centers in New York and New Jersey, with plans on foot for the renovation of buildings and improvements to property, this Seminary is at the threshold of one of the brightest periods in its long and honored history.[3]

One of the reasons for Dr. Demarest's reluctance to present the synod of 1925 with a name to fill the new chair of religious education was the fact that he wanted to try out his candidate first. During the academic year 1925-6 Demarest brought to the campus Dr. William A. Weber who had been teaching the subject at Bonebrake Seminary in Dayton, Ohio. A minister in the United Brethren Church, Dr. Weber had studied at Berlin and Marburg and ultimately received his doctorate from Yale. The year's trial was satisfactory and Dr. Weber's name was presented to the synod of 1926 which elected him without dissent.

After the Worcester battle of a few years earlier, one may wonder at the ease with which the appointment of Dr. Weber, another outsider, was approved. After all, Dr. Weber came from a tradition much more Arminian than that of Dr. Worcester! One can only assume that, rightly or wrongly, religious education was considered a much less sensitive area than theology. There is the additional fact that Dr. Weber had very impressive credentials in his field, which was a relatively new one, while Dr. Worcester was a pastor-theologian, which just about every Reformed Church domine considered himself to be.

Dr. Weber's coming to the campus as the sixth professor raised a problem in housing, for which Dr. Demarest had provided by a land transaction on Bishop Place. The board purchased the former home of Professor Bevier of Rutgers in exchange for a piece of land on the same street, on which Professor Bevier's daughter proposed to build a new home (now the provost's office of Rutgers). Unhappily, the home was not satisfactory to the Webers, who spent all of their years at New Brunswick in the apartment in Hertzog Hall where Dr. Weber had lived during his trial year.

When Dr. Gillespie was unable to continue his lectorship, the seminary secured the services of Dr. Louis H. Holden, at that time the pastor of Second Reformed Church. When Dr. Holden gave up the Second Church pastorate in 1925, he signified his willingness to continue as lector at New Brunswick. Ultimately, he moved into the house that had belonged to Professor Bevier.

Dr. Holden continued his lectorship until 1941 and proved to be a valuable adjunct to the seminary's biblical department.

Another major change was made in 1926 in the rules governing the bachelor of divinity degree. Coming into line with standard practice, the seminary voted to grant the degree to any college graduate who had completed the full seminary curriculum, including the original languages. This new policy became operative with the class of 1926. Graduates from previous years could obtain the degree with eight additional hours of supervised work at the seminary. For those in the post-graduate programs, the same amount of work which had formerly earned a bachelor of divinity degree would now earn the degree of master of theology. All of these new arrangements were made with the consent of the trustees of Rutgers College, who still awarded the degrees at the recommendation of the seminary faculty.

Matters continued to improve during the next few years. The enrollment at the seminary began to increase, while enrollment in the post-graduate courses continued fairly constant. Students who just a few years before had been complaining bitterly about the faculty now asked to have some of the faculty's lectures published in permanent form. Both Dr. Demarest and Dr. Raven published books, the first on the Reformed Church *Constitution* and the second on the history of religion in Israel. Competent lecturers in a variety of fields were brought to the seminary to supplement the regular course of instruction.

Moneys were obtained for a complete renovation of Hertzog Hall and some of the other buildings on campus. Dr. Demarest's growing list of "friends of New Brunswick Seminary" contributed annually to its budget. Dr. Raven, who had some private means, received permission to build his own home on seminary land on Bishop Place, with the understanding that eventually the house would revert to the seminary. Best of all, the Pell estate, one which had involved litigation for about two decades, seemed to be near settlement. From it, the school expected to receive nearly $150,000—a hope that revived talk about the long-needed completion of the library.

Dr. Van Dyke, who had served as librarian since 1878, was in increasingly poor health, so that for the past few years his title had been largely an honorific one. The real librarian had been Dr. Worcester, who with Dr. Beardslee as his colleague on the Library Committee, managed the operation. Dr. Worcester, in fact, had been named as associate librarian. He undertook the complete rearrangement of the books in the library, moving some to the basement where new shelving was provided, doing away with the double rows of books on the shelves, reclassifying many of the volumes, and bringing the catalogue up-to-date. Quite possibly, Dr. Worcester's management of the library and the many hours which he spent on it may have been his greatest contribution to the seminary.

In 1928 a question arose as to the wisdom of incorporating the school. Western had been a corporation for some years, but at New Brunswick the only corporation was a New York one, the denominational Board of Direction. Several times this anomaly had proved to be an embarrassment in settling estates, and with the impending settlement of the Pell estate it became a live question again. General Synod gave its consent in 1928, and New Brunswick Seminary, though it had existed in the state since 1810, became a New Jersey corporation in 1929.

The Reformed Church in America celebrated its tercentennial in 1928 and while most of the celebration took place in New York, the seminary took an active part in it. The 300th anniversary of the Reformed Church in America found a school that once again could hold its head high as a significant and important part of the life of the church. Much smaller now than its sister school in Holland, Michigan, New Brunswick was nonetheless pioneering in several new and important areas in providing an adequate ministry for the Reformed Church in the rapidly-changing areas of the Northeast.

The report for 1929 was a glowing one. Student enrollment had risen to thirty-one, and there were fifty-nine others enrolled in the continuing education programs, which by now had four centers—New Brunswick, New York, Albany, and Kingston. Fac-

ulty salaries had been increased to $4,000 a year; the Donors'
Fund enjoyed a healthy growth. Best of all, the first construction
in many a year was taking place on Holy Hill. A smaller building,
under construction behind Suydam Hall, was a duplex house for
furloughing missionaries. A larger project was the long-dreamed-
of-completion of Lienau's original design for Gardner Sage Library. Two transepts and an apse were being added. The transepts, at a cost of $80,000, were provided by the Pell estate. The
apse was provided by a special bequest of Mrs. Cornelia Van Pelt
for $11,000. The new buildings were to be known as the Wessells
Memorial Building, for Mrs. Pell's family, and the Gilbert Van
Pelt Alcove, for Mrs. Van Pelt's late husband. As Dr. Worcester
said,

> It is a gratefully expectant Library staff which notes the clink of the
> trowel and the hammer.[4]

The seminary had indeed come a long way since the dark days
of 1922 and 1923. In all the euphoria of 1929, who could have
predicted the bitter time that was coming to the country and its
effect on the life of the school?

The consequences of the disastrous stock market crash of October, 1929, were not immediately felt in the seminary, as was
true in many parts of the country. In 1930 all programs were
operating, many improvements were being made on the property, and books were being moved into the new Wessells addition
to the library, which provided space for 40,000 additional volumes. Endowment income was actually a little larger than it had
been because the balance of the Pell estate had been invested.
Dr. Raven was doing part-time teaching at Princeton, as he had
for several years. Dr. Beardslee was on a four-month leave of
absence, doing foreign mission deputation work, but the seminary had been fortunate to secure the celebrated Dr. James Mof-
fat of Union as his replacement. Dr. Bayles was developing a
field work program in the Practical Theology Department. Miss
Margaret Wilson had become the new assistant librarian.

The only change which affected the future was the decision to have only one commencement speaker. Hitherto there had been two—one representing the superintendents and the other the alumni. Beginning with the commencement service of 1931, it was decided that there should be only one speaker, "not necessarily from the ministers of our own denomination, to be selected and secured by the Faculty, the President of the Board of Superintendents, and the President of the Alumni Association to be consulted by the Faculty in making this choice."[5]

The first signs of cracks in the plaster because of the growing depression came in 1931 when the Board of Directors (as the Board of Managers had come to be known) reported that total receipts for the year "have been substantially less than last year, chiefly due to lessened income from the endowment funds."[6] The year had closed with a deficit of about $3,000, but no one seemed unduly worried about it. So far as students were concerned, the entering class of fourteen had been the largest in twenty years. With thirty-two students enrolled at the seminary and fifty others in the four post-graduate programs, the outlook seemed very bright indeed.

With the death of Dr. John C. Van Dyke on December 5, 1932, an era came to an end. Associated with Gardner Sage Library since 1878, in more recent years he had largely confined his attention to the fine arts collection which was his first love, while the burden of the day-to-day operation of the main library fell on Dr. Worcester and Miss Wilson. With Van Dyke's death, the seminary lost its most legendary figure, as well in the larger New Brunswick community as in the school. As a sign of the times, the house which he had occupied in George Street was, after his death, remodeled to become two apartments for married students!

It was just about at this time that the seminary acquired a man who was to become another legendary figure—the Rev. Edward H. Bishop. Having retired from the ministry and moved to New Brunswick, Bishop volunteered his services in the library. However, after a short time he was put in charge of the museum.

Hundreds of people who were children in New Brunswick at the time remember the programs which Mr. Bishop planned for them in the museum after school and on Saturdays. His was a unique ministry which related the seminary to the community in a way that had not happened previously.

For some years the alumni had contributed the necessary funds to provide several lectures on preaching, given by distinguished occupants of American pulpits. In the academic year 1932-3 their funding extended to make it possible for Dr. George Buttrick of the Madison Avenue Presbyterian Church in New York to come to the seminary for a ten-week course in preaching, offered on Mondays to middlers and seniors.

Financial problems forced the discontinuance in 1933 of all centers of the post-graduate program except New Brunswick, which still enrolled twenty-five students. Another possible reason for giving up the work in Albany, Kingston, and New York was that almost the entire faculty was involved in the School for Christian Leaders which was held under the sponsorship of the Middlesex County Council of Religious Education. One hundred thirty students, most of them Sunday school teachers, were enrolled for the five sessions which were held at the seminary.

Ever since 1932 a committee had been working on plans for the celebration of the 150th anniversary of New Brunswick Seminary. The actual celebration was held on Tuesday and Wednesday, October 2 and 3, 1934. The celebration began on Tuesday afternoon with addresses given by Dr. Worcester and President George Richards of Lancaster Seminary. A reception and a dinner were followed by an evening session at which Drs. Frederic Berg and Samuel Zwemer spoke on the seminary's contribution to the church and the mission field.

On Wednesday morning an academic procession went from Holy Hill to Kirkpatrick Chapel on the Rutgers campus, where a special service of thanksgiving was held and at which Dr. Demarest gave a historical address. About fifty colleges and seminaries were represented in the procession. The closing event was a luncheon held in the Rutgers Gymnasium and attended by approximately 350 people. The speaker at the luncheon was Dr. Albert Beaven, president of Colgate Seminary and one of the recognized leaders in the field of American theological education.

The class of 1934 was the first class to receive degrees from New Brunswick Seminary. Arrangements had been made during the previous year with the Rutgers trustees and the educational authorities of the State of New Jersey for New Brunswick to offer its own degrees in divinity instead of referring them to Rutgers. Though the change represented another break in the long history of relations between New Brunswick Seminary and Rutgers, it was seen as a fitting way to celebrate the seminary's 150th anniversary. The five men who received the bachelor of divinity degree in 1934 and the four who received the minister of theology degree were literally the first degree graduates in the history of New Brunswick Seminary.

In spite of the festivities, however, the financial picture continued to deteriorate. The income on endowments dropped drastically as did gifts from congregations and donors. Only a couple of generous gifts from individuals spared the treasurer from reaching more deeply into the school's limited reserve funds. Faculty salaries, already reduced by ten percent, were cut by one-third. Library acquisitions were kept to a minimum. It was not a happy time for those responsible for the financial health of any educational enterprise.

There were some bright spots in the gloom, however. It was learned that the Rev. Abraham Messler Quick of the class of 1864 had left the seminary $60,000 toward the endowment of the chair of church history, while from the estate of the late John Bussing an unknown but generous amount would be paid into the seminary's coffers.

With the celebration of the 150th anniversary, President Demarest decided that the time had come for him to make way for a successor. Already past his seventy-first birthday, he felt that the strains and stresses imposed by the Great Depression called for someone younger and more energetic, even though because of his residence in the old Cook House on Seminary Place he would continue to be a presence on the seminary campus.

Dr. Demarest's resignation, as of December 31, 1934, was accepted with great regret. In the ten years that he had headed the seminary, its whole situation both externally and internally had vastly changed for the better. The minutes of the Board of Directors give an accurate summary of what the Demarest decade had done for New Brunswick.

> The ten years during which he administered the affairs of the Seminary had been years of signal progress. At the very beginning of his term of office Hertzog Hall was renovated inside and out. The Library building has been doubled in size and more than doubled in usableness. A house for the occupancy of two missionary families was erected and has been continuously occupied. A vacant lot owned by the Seminary was without additional expense exchanged for a house and lot . . . As an executive Dr. Demarest's service has been unique. He found a group of professors each pursuing his own way and showed us how to work together as a unit . . . His care of the finances has been minute, watchful and of singular clarity and foresight. The creation and maintenance of the Donor's Fund has enabled the Seminary widely to extend its usefulness . . . Students and professors alike will not soon forget the generous hospitality of his home, so frequently renewed.[7]

X

In Sunshine and Storm

Because Dr. Demarest's resignation at the end of 1934 had come
with little advance warning, the directors of the seminary had no
immediate candidate for his successor. They naturally turned to
Dr. John W. Beardslee, Jr., professor of New Testament, who
had been Dr. Demarest's loyal colleague in administering seminary affairs, to serve as acting president while the whole question
of the office was discussed.

The problem was that when Dr. Demarest had become the
first president of New Brunswick Seminary in 1925, he was already in semi-retirement. Since he had a very small teaching load
at the school, he was able to give virtually full-time service in
administration and public relations. He had thus set a rigorous
pattern for any successor to follow. Well versed in the history of
the Dutch Church, Demarest had been greatly in demand as a
preacher on anniversary occasions in local congregations, as well
as at academic gatherings. All of his activity had greatly strengthened the image of the seminary in the mind of the Reformed
Church.

But the straitened finances of the seminary hardly permitted
the selection of a full-time president, even if someone of Dr.
Demarest's caliber could be found. On the other hand, if a full-
time member of the faculty were chosen to the office, would it
be fair to expect him to carry all of these administrative duties in
addition to his teaching responsibilities? While the board discussed this issue, Dr. Beardslee began to demonstrate that the
combination was indeed possible. Even if he could not carry on
with all of Dr. Demarest's outside engagements, he made himself
useful in a number of other directions, and his quiet efficiency
soon endeared him to students and board members alike.

John W. Beardslee, Jr.

The year 1935 was probably the lowest point in the seminary's financial affairs in many years. The $888,000 endowment held for the seminary by the Board of Direction had in 1929 yielded an income of $45,000; in 1935 it produced $16,000, or a return of two percent. As the report of the Committee on the Board of Direction indicated in 1936, that board had made heavy investments in New York real estate mortgages with rather disastrous results.

> . . . the Board of Direction . . . has continued the policy of placing the props against the endowment structure in an endeavor to save the principal of the moneys entrusted to it. This policy is one of necessity, caused by the investment of large sums of money in real estate mortgages. To save the principal, many pieces of property have been taken over by foreclosure or deed, with added expenditures to keep standing the original investments. In these properties some $275,000 was invested, and recently in the program of foreclosure, to save the original outlay, some $45,000 has been expended as props.[1]

The committee went so far as to recommend that a special committee be appointed to investigate the possibility of dissolving the Board of Direction and returning the money to the various agencies and institutions for which it was acting. Such a committee was in fact appointed but was never able to come to any conclusion in the matter.

In the meantime, however, since its incorporation in 1929, the seminary had quietly been holding some small estates, which together with other balances totaled approximately $20,000, a sum which it had invested at a much better rate of interest. That sum, together with gifts from churches and individual donors, and a special drive among the alumni (which had yielded $487.50), meant that the seminary was able to balance its austerity budget of $36,818! And it was an austerity budget! Not only was the library staff reduced to one person (with some assistance from student wives), but all special lectureships were discontinued, and every repair that was not drastically necessary was deferred. Even the seminary basketball team was suspended! Faculty members were asked to take a voluntary pay cut of twenty-five percent, to which they all assented. As a small token of concern, General Synod included the sum of $1,200 for both schools in the synodical assessment, an action which was continued for the next several years.

It is not surprising that classes reacted in a variety of ways. Two classes, Paramus and Ulster, overtured the synod of 1936 to combine the two schools, while two others, Dakota and Germania, sent in overtures requesting that all faculty salaries be made a matter of General Synod assessment. Needless to say, nothing came of any of these overtures, but they indicated that the future of both New Brunswick and Western seminaries was a matter of wide concern in the Reformed Church in America.

Having experienced an acting president who could guide the fortunes of the seminary through such troublous times, the Board of Directors recommended to the synod of 1936 that Dr. Beardslee be elected president of New Brunswick Seminary, a motion which the synod adopted by a unanimous standing vote. The language of the board's motion is worth quoting.

His gifts and qualifications for his high office are well known to the members of Synod and the Church at large. We love to think of him as an honored son of an honored father. His gifts have been demonstrated most admirably in the past year in the arrangement of the curriculum, his leadership in the faculty, his marked influence with the students, and his ability in financial planning for the Seminary's needs . . .

Despite his modesty in all things, we know he will bring successfully to the office the spirit of consecration, wisdom and prayerfulness that is characteristic of all that he does. We confidently recommend him to you in the hope that you will give him back to us as the spiritual leader of your Seminary in New Brunswick.[2]

Lest it be thought that the Board of Directors took a long time to decide that the acting president should become president, it should be pointed out that there was no session of the General Synod in 1935. By common consent it had been decided to omit any session that year because of the depression. No doubt the board would have been ready with a recommendation that June, but there could be no election.

During his long interim, however, Dr. Beardslee had been acting as full president. An honors system was instituted in the curriculum for students able to undertake greater academic responsibilities, a new system of comprehensive examinations was begun for all seniors, and extra tutorials were offered by some faculty members to help supplement the curriculum.

The question of making Hebrew an elective, which had been raised from time to time in the past, came on the agenda again at the General Synod of 1937. It was decided to survey the ministers of the Reformed Church for an answer to the question. By 1938 it was known that 407 of them felt that Hebrew should be a required subject, while only 276 believed that it should be made an elective. On that basis Hebrew remained in the seminary's curriculum.

A real blow fell on the seminary with the unexpected death of Dr. Worcester on June 25, 1937. His death was keenly felt by the entire seminary community, and in the fall of that year the

alumni voted to raise a sum of money to renovate the chapel in
Hertzog Hall in his memory. The services of Clement Fair-
weather, an architect from Metuchen, New Jersey, were secured,
and what had been a somewhat dingy room was redesigned as a
handsome chapel in the colonial style. The new facility, now
called Worcester Chapel, was completed in 1938 at a cost of
$5,000. While there were some donations from friends of Dr.
Worcester's, the bulk of the money was raised by gifts from former students. In all, over 300 people contributed to make possible the new Worcester Chapel.

As a sign of the times, it should be noted that by 1937 the two
apartments in Van Dyke House were no longer sufficient for the
number of married students attending the seminary. Two new
apartments, each renting for $53 a month, were therefore created
on the first floor of one of the wings of Hertzog Hall.

Dr. Beardslee did not move immediately to fill the vacancy
which had occurred by reason of Dr. Worcester's death. During
the academic year 1937-8 a number of visitors took the classes in
theology, including Professor Edwin Lewis of Drew, whose recent espousal of the theology of Karl Barth had shaken the Meth-
odist world. In 1938 Dr. Beardslee recommended the appointment
of Norman Victor Hope of Scotland, for one semester. An honors
graduate of Edinburgh who had done graduate study in Berlin,
Mr. Hope came with high commendation from Dr. John Baillie
of the Edinburgh divinity faculty.

Was it in response to the announcement of Mr. Hope's appointment to the synod of 1938 that Dr. Harry Hager submitted
the following motion to the meeting

Resolved
1) That the General Synod express its mind that our Seminaries shall
   refrain from employing for lectureships and part time teaching
   those whose theological views are not in complete harmony with
   the confessional standards of our Reformed Church;
2) That the General Synod urge the governing bodies of both Seminaries, if at all possible, to secure those from our own denomination to fill the present vacancies in our Seminaries.[3]

Another vacancy in the faculty occurred in 1938. On December 17, after a forty-year association with New Brunswick Seminary, Dr. Raven offered his resignation as professor of Old Testament. He had hoped to remain with the school until the mandatory retirement age of seventy, but his rapidly deteriorating eyesight had made that impossible. Despite the long period of his tenure, Dr. Raven remained a popular member of the faculty right to the end. Once again a variety of "neighbors" had to be asked to help in the interim, including Dr. Charles Fritsch of Princeton.

About this time the financial situation of the school was eased somewhat by the receipt of an estate of $60,000 from the late Judge Frech. Judge Frech's estate was added to the moneys held and was invested in New Brunswick, since the income of the Endowment Fund held in New York had risen only to 2.2 percent! Partly because of the receipt of the Frech estate and partly because contributions from local churches had begun to rise, the General Synod in 1940 no longer contributed to the seminary from the assessment fund.

One of the reasons why enrollment at the seminary continued to rise during these years (It had numbered twenty-three when Dr. Beardslee took over the presidency, and by 1940 had reached thirty-seven.) was the very impressive list of adjunct faculty which the administration had been able to secure. Dr. George Buttrick of the Madison Avenue Presbyterian Church in New York, Dr. Joseph Sizoo of St. Nicholas Collegiate, and Dr. Norman Vincent Peale of the Marble Collegiate took turns offering a course in homiletics each year. Dr. Milton Stauffer of the neighboring Second Reformed Church offered a course in missions, while courses in social Christianity were offered alternately by Oscar Maddaus of Manhasset and Abraham J. Muste of the Labor Temple in New York. Donald Wheeler of Princeton Seminary regularly gave instruction in speech. The presence of these regular visitors to the campus greatly enriched the curricular offerings of the school and attracted new students.

In the meantime, however, the evening extension program at

New Brunswick was given up in 1939, and the last minister of
theology degree was awarded by the institution in that year also.
One of the reasons for abandoning what had been a very successful program was the rise of lay schools in many parts of the
church. Evidently, Dr. Beardslee felt that the use of faculty for
this purpose was a more profitable investment of faculty time
than was the extension program.

It was in 1940 that the celebrated Dutch carillon which had
been in the Netherlands Building at the 1939 World's Fair was
installed in the cupola of Hertzog Hall. The bells had been cast
by the van Bergen bell foundry in Holland; the installation was
their first in America. Through his Dutch connections, Dr. Hoffman had secured the bells when the building was dismantled at
the end of the fair, and a gift from Mr. Joseph Rainey of St.
Johnsville, New York, took care of the cost of moving the carillon
to New Brunswick and installing it in Hertzog Hall.

Dr. Bayles, who had served as professor of practical theology
since 1924, reached the mandatory retirement age in the summer
of 1941 and therefore tendered his resignation. Arrangements
were made with Dr. M. Stephen James, pastor of the First Church
in Albany, New York, to spend Monday afternoons and Tuesday
mornings on the campus, teaching courses in homiletics, liturgics,
and administration, and holding personal interviews with the students. In the meantime, Dr. Bayles continued to direct student
appointments and summer assignments.

Seminary personnel was further disturbed by the decision of
Dr. Holden to retire in 1941. Never a permanent member of the
faculty, he had served as lector in English Bible since 1924 and
had made a valuable contribution to the life of the school. Dr.
Holden was not replaced; his duties were divided between Dr.
Beardslee and the Rev. J. Coert Rylaarsdam, a recent graduate
of the seminary, who had returned at the beginning of 1941 to
serve as an instructor in Old Testament.

Although he had had to fill three vacancies during the first few
years of his presidency, Dr. Beardslee had been successful in
each case. He always proceeded cautiously by making a tempo-

rary appointment at the outset. Only after a trial period was the new faculty person presented to General Synod for election. Having tried this method in the case of Mr. Hope, who was elected by the synod in 1939, Dr. Beardslee was obviously using it again for both Dr. James and Mr. Rylaarsdam.

The synod of 1942 elected both Dr. James and Mr. Rylaarsdam to the professorate, thus giving the seminary a full faculty for the first time in several years. Everything about the life of the seminary seemed to be gaining. Enrollment had risen to forty-three, generous donors had provided funds for necessary renovation of the buildings, and two houses in Bishop Place had been purchased for investment purposes. The final settlement of the estate of John Bussing had added approximately $100,000 to the seminary endowment, and it had finally been decided that the income should be used for a John Bussing Chair of Preaching and Practical Theology.

Only one small item in the reports for 1942 indicates anything about the effect of the world situation on the seminary at that time: one of the students was appointed air raid warden for that part of New Brunswick in which the seminary was located. That, apparently, was the seminary's introduction to a whole series of calamities in which Pearl Harbor and our entry into the Second World War were to involve it. That involvement was to be felt on a physical level in terms of the impossibility of finding men to keep the seminary's grounds and buildings in order and in the rapidly increasing maintenance costs. It was to be felt in relatively minor ways, such as the government order to convert the heating system in Hertzog Hall from oil back to coal. All building maintenance fell on one man, with such student volunteers as he could find.

The effects on the life of the school were even more disruptive. For one thing, the student body was divided between those who took a pacifist position and those who supported the cause of the Allied powers. Members of the faculty were also divided at this point. The result was that offerings at chapel services were divided between war relief and support of conscientious objectors, with some students and faculty refusing to give to whichever cause they disapproved. The divisions of those years most likely provided an excellent training ground in Christian forgiveness and reconciliation for the entire seminary community, but they took their toll in terms of the peace and unity of Holy Hill.

The most serious effect of the war, however, was in the whole question of student enrollment, which had reached a high point of fifty-one in the fall of 1942, slipping back to forty-six the following year. The Selective Service Board, which originally had provided deferments for college students intending to enter seminary, began to tighten its restrictions in 1944. A ruling in April of that year required that all college students intending to enter seminary must be matriculated in some seminary by July 1, or face immediate induction into the armed forces.

Such a ruling made fewer problems for Roman Catholic seminaries than it did for Protestant ones, which had always required a college degree as the basis for admission to seminary. As a partial response to the new ruling the Association of Theological Schools allowed seminaries to admit students who had finished three-fourths of their college work, although it was understood that no divinity degree could be awarded until the bachelor's degree had been obtained.

That concession, however, merely postponed the inevitable. New Brunswick accepted students on the basis allowed by the association and instituted a complete summer semester to accelerate the program of theological education. The problem began to be felt in 1945 when a graduating class of sixteen was replaced by an entering class of eight, five of whom had been involved in the summer program. Not only was the enrollment of the school likely to be cut in half, but a stringent application of the rules of the selective service could mean there would be no pre-seminary students in colleges a few years hence. It took little prescience to understand why a student enrollment which had numbered fifty-one in 1943 was down to twenty-eight just four years later. The fact that college students who were certified candidates for seminary were not allowed to complete their college course, but were subject to the draft, had taken its inevitable toll in seminary enrollment.

In the years after the war the financial problems of the school, due to inflation, were more pressing than they had been before. The interest rate from the Board of Direction investments was theoretically better because the board had reduced the book value of the seminary's endowment from $900,000 to $675,000, but that put no more money in the till. Dr. Hoffman was laboring heroically to secure contributions from churches, but by 1946 these amounted only to a little more than $12,000. The increased contributions did little more than offset the inflated cost of living, especially when faculty salaries had to be raised to $4,500 a year just to keep up with inflation.

Personnel changes also took place during this difficult time. Dr. Rylaarsdam submitted his resignation in 1945 to accept a position with the divinity school in the University of Chicago, from which he had just obtained his doctorate. It was an invitation which he had rejected several times before he finally accepted it. While it was flattering to New Brunswick to have one of its faculty members invited to such a celebrated school, his leaving left a large gap in the New Brunswick community. A year later Professor Hope resigned and accepted an invitation to join the faculty of Princeton Seminary. Just prior to this, there had been a student complaint circulated in the Board of Superintendents, alleging incompetence and inefficiency on the part of most faculty members, so that there was great reluctance to find replacements in either Old Testament or theology. Dr. Julius Bewer, who had just retired from the faculty of Union Seminary, was asked to serve as interim professor of Old Testament, while the Rev. Justin Vander Kolk, a graduate of the seminary who had entered the ministry of the Congregational Church, accepted a position as instructor in theology.

For some time Dr. Beardslee had considered asking for relief from his administrative duties so that he could give full time to study and teaching. On January 28, 1947, he informed the superintendents and directors that his resignation as president would become effective as of March 1. The burdens of administration, with all the problems of a falling enrollment, financial constraints, faculty vacancies, and student unrest, were more than he wanted to live with for the remaining two years of his time at New Brunswick Seminary. He longed for nothing but the classroom and his own study.

The lasting achievements of President Beardslee's almost twelve years in office should not be forgotten. At the expense of much deferred maintenance, he had developed a strong faculty with a fine supplement of adjuncts, and he had allowed nothing to hinder the development of Gardner Sage Library as one of the finest theological libraries in the country. One of his last acts was to authorize the sale of Audubon's *Birds*, which Sage had himself presented to the library, so that various books on theology and history, which a lack of funds had prevented the school from purchasing, could be added to the seminary's holdings.

The fact that Dr. Beardslee's successor was waiting in the wings makes one wonder whether weariness was the only factor involved in his resignation. The imbroglio which ensued when the Collegiate consistory discussed the possibility of selling St. Nicholas Church at Fifth Avenue and Forty-Eighth Street in New York had made Joseph R. Sizoo, already a prince of the American pulpit, virtually a national figure. The meeting of January 28, 1947, which received Dr. Beardslee's resignation was also informed that Dr. Sizoo was willing to become acting president of New Brunswick on March 1 and to be elected to the office at the next meeting of General Synod.

Dr. Sizoo had indicated to the board that he would be willing to serve without salary, but that he expected to be provided with housing. He also intended to bring his secretary from New York and expected the seminary to provide her with a salary. These terms were acceptable and Dr. Sizoo in time moved into the home occupied by Dr. James. This was the first break in assigning faculty housing in terms of the field of teaching. Dr. James moved into one of the houses in Bishop Place, which the seminary had

Joseph R. Sizoo

purchased a few years earlier and which had been rented as an investment.

The new president began his term of office in a whirlwind of activity. Much in demand as a lecturer and a preacher in all parts of the country, Dr. Sizoo spent enough time at the seminary to see Hertzog Hall completely redecorated both without and within, to sponsor several recruiting events, and to visit several prospective donors to the Endowment Fund. Even though during his first year the student body numbered only twenty-four and the budget deficit was the largest in history, the board was convinced that the future was bright with promise. It wanted to give the lie to "the untrue report circulated in certain sections of the Church that the Seminary will soon close." Even though most of its hopes still had to be realized, the board was convinced that under Dr.

Sizoo's dynamic leadership, the seminary's brightest days were still to come.

Dr. Sizoo's first appointment was that of the Rev. Dr. Hugh Baillie MacLean to fill the vacancy in Old Testament which Dr. Bewer had been filling. A native of Scotland and a graduate of St. Andrew's University in both arts and theology, Dr. MacLean had received the doctor of theology degree from Union Seminary in New York. Indeed, it may very well have been Dr. Bewer who first called Dr. Sizoo's attention to him. At the time of his coming to New Brunswick in the fall of 1947, MacLean was chaplain of the Moral Leadership School in Jerusalem, having previously served a parish in Scotland.

After a year's service as instructor, Dr. MacLean was recommended to the General Synod of 1948 for election as Gardner Sage Professor of Old Testament. Almost as though it expected the coming storm, in presenting Dr. MacLean's name the Board of Superintendents said

> He is thoroughly sound in his position on Reformed Church doctrine and subscribes to all the doctrines of our church without any reservation including the doctrine of inspiration, the doctrine of grace, the doctrine of the Incarnation and the Virgin Birth. He has read and studied the canons of the church and accepts them. He is evangelical in his position.[4]

No opposition was offered at the time of election, but it was a certainty that those who had supported the Hager resolution of 1938 were watching for their first opportunity to embarrass New Brunswick and its new professor of Old Testament. Their opportunity was not long in coming. Dr. MacLean was installed in his office at the Fall Alumni Convocation in 1948. During his inaugural address he said that in saying that God had commanded the extermination of the Canaanites, the Hebrews had "falsified" history in the interests of their theology. That single word was enough to unleash all of the forces which had been waiting to get at New Brunswick Seminary for some time.

When the General Synod met in 1949 it was confronted by no fewer than thirty-three communications on the MacLean affair. Thirteen of these were from classes and particular synods (all in the Middle West), asking that the theological position of Dr. MacLean be further investigated. Seventeen (all from classes and particular synods in the East) of the communications expressed confidence in Dr. MacLean and in the New Brunswick faculty. The remaining overtures expressed disapproval of the way in which the columns of *The Church Herald* (formerly *The Christian Intelligencer*) had been used almost to try the case in the public press. The committee had also received a letter from the Board of Directors, as well as a statement which the professor had prepared for the Board of Superintendents.

Synod's Committee on Professorate, the chairman of which was the Rev. Peter Muyskens of Hamilton, Michigan, went at the question in a very deliberate way.

> After having familiarized ourselves with Dr. MacLean's written statement, we invited him to our committee meeting and he gave us an oral explanation covering the several items in greater detail. Next we invited in representatives of the Classes which had sent in overtures and read Dr. MacLean's written statement to them to discover whether or not his statement replied to the points called for in the overtures. Later still we invited Dr. Sizoo to discuss the matter with us.[5]

After following these procedures, the committee voted to recommend an expression of confidence in Professor MacLean and New Brunswick Seminary, a recommendation which was overwhelmingly adopted.

It could be called a case of "all's well that ends well," but the cost to the seminary in emotional energy and public relations was considerable. The faculties of both New Brunswick and Western had incurred some wrath a year earlier when they had issued a joint statement on the membership of the Reformed Church in the then Federal Council of Churches. The MacLean affair, though it had certainly been inadvertently triggered, was a further impediment to good relations between the seminary and the churches. It took all of Dr. Sizoo's skill in public relations (which was not inconsiderable) to calm the storm and pour oil on the troubled waters.

It should be said that in spite of this troubled beginning, Dr. MacLean soon proved to be one of the most valuable and most popular members of the faculty. The warmth of his Scottish personality and the strength of his personal convictions endeared him to the generation of those who studied with him, and his efforts on behalf of the school were tireless.

Almost lost in all the excitement of the MacLean affair was the fact that in 1949 Dr. Beardslee reached the mandatory retirement age of seventy. One of the reasons why so little notice was taken of it at the time was that it made almost no difference in his relationship with the seminary. Dr. Sizoo did not intend to lose the services of one of the finest members of his faculty. Although Dr. Beardslee ceased to be a General Synod professor that year, he continued to teach New Testament at the seminary by invitation of the administration and in fact was named dean.

Almost equally unnoticed was the fact that under Dr. Sizoo's leadership the seminary was beginning to pull out of its decline. A student body which had numbered only twenty-four when he came in 1947 had by 1949 risen to thirty-four. Finances continued to be a nagging problem. Having been assigned a generous share in the denomination's United Advance Fund, the seminary had gone ahead with extensive plans for the very necessary renovation of its plant, only to discover that the failure of the fund to reach its goal meant that the seminary received much less than expected. Some of the plans could be canceled, but others were for such essential items that the school dipped into its reserves to carry them to completion. Dr. Sizoo was fortunate in having as his treasurer the Rev. Dr. A. L. Warnshuis, the retired secretary of the International Missionary Council and an alumnus of the seminary. Not only were Dr. Warnshuis's financial skills great, but he was well connected with possible sources of increased revenue for the seminary.

In the summer of 1950 another member of the old guard of the faculty, William A. Weber, reached retirement age and was relieved of his duties as professor. The beginning of the academic year in the fall of 1950 saw two experiments with the curriculum. Instead of the traditional two-semester plan the faculty voted to change to the newer plan of three terms, which at that time was a growing academic fashion. Recognizing the need to attract students from other denominations, the faculty that fall also began to offer an alternate route to the bachelor of divinity degree, which eliminated the original languages for students from denominations in which they were no longer a requirement.

Some of the fruits of these new directions became apparent that very fall. A bumper entering class of twenty-one lifted the total student population to fifty-four. By 1951 the financial situation was bright enough to warrant raising faculty salaries to $5,000.

The synod of 1951 also elected two men to fill the vacancies then existing on the faculty. For the chair of Christian education, which had been vacated by Dr. Weber's retirement a year earlier, Dr. Herbert Van Wyk, professor of Bible at Central College in Pella was chosen. Dr. Van Wyk had come to the seminary in the fall of 1950 to serve as instructor and on the basis of his acceptance was elected a professor. Ever since Dr. Hope had gone to Princeton Seminary in 1946 the James Suydam Chair of Systematic Theology had been vacant. For five years the Rev. Justin Vander Kolk had been serving as instructor in theology. Now that his doctorate at Chicago was virtually completed, he was nominated and elected to the full professorate in 1951.

It is worth noting in passing the way in which the policy of faculty selection at New Brunswick had quietly fallen into line with that of American theological education generally. In the not too distant past no one would have been kept as an instructor for five years pending the completion of his doctorate, but an earned degree in every field except practical theology was now standard for accreditation by the Association of Theological Schools. It had doubtless been Dr. Beardslee who had first insisted that this standard be met in selections for the New Brunswick faculty.

A revised plan of seminary organization was also adopted in 1951. It was basically similar to that which had been adopted in 1923. What had been the Board of Directors was now to be known as the Executive Committee, nominated by the superintendents and elected by General Synod. In other respects it pretty much followed the previous plan, except for drawing up more specific committee responsibilities for the superintendents.

A much healthier financial picture encouraged the seminary to present a budget of $77,430 to the church for 1952, which included $41,430 in gifts from congregations. Since this represented more than a doubling of current contributions, it was indeed an act of faith. An even greater act of faith was the plan to launch a special fund-raising drive for $150,000 to put the persistent problem of buildings and grounds to rest. The largest part of the money to be raised was $53,000 for repairing and redecorating faculty homes, which were all in deplorable condition. A large sum was also allocated for reconstructing the driveways on the campus. Every building was to receive some attention, including the creation of four additional apartments in Hertzog Hall for married students.

A large shadow was cast across all these plans by the knowledge that Dr. Sizoo was likely to leave his office in 1952. From the time of his arrival at the seminary in 1947 he had always spoken in terms of a five-year presidency, but no one had taken him seriously. Indeed there was a persistent rumor that a New York foundation had provided the funding for a five-year salary, but this was never stated openly. While many hopes were held to the contrary, President Sizoo announced that he would resign his office in June of 1952.

Dr. Sizoo's accomplishments in five years had been sizeable. Not only had student enrollment reached one of its peaks, but there was a largely new and enthusiastic faculty to attract them. Partly as a result of the aftermaths of the MacLean controversy, the seminary had a new, closer relationship with the congregations of the three eastern synods. Churches were beginning to assume larger responsibilities for the school's finances. The introduction of an annual Seminary Sunday in October had served to focus attention on the financial needs of the institution, and the launching of the $150,000 drive promised to bring to an end the continuing worry about deteriorating buildings.

The foundations had been laid for some successful years, but Dr. Sizoo left before he could build on them. If the school was to move forward, the choice of a new president was crucial.

XI

The Old Order Changes

Even though Dr. Sizoo had from the beginning indicated that he intended to serve only five years as president of New Brunswick Seminary, the resignation which he submitted on July 1, 1952, seemed to take everyone by surprise. Evidently it had been thought that the success which the school was enjoying under his administration would persuade him to change his mind. Student enrollment was now nearing sixty, and the seminary was enjoying new confidence in terms of support from the churches.

The continuing problem was a nagging financial one. During the last year of Dr. Sizoo's administration, the seminary incurred one of its greatest deficits, over $19,000, largely because some of the crying needs of the physical plant simply had to be met. The real disappointment, however, was that contributions from churches continued at about $20,000, despite repeated appeals for at least twice that much to balance the budget.

When Dr. Sizoo left the seminary presidency, the board asked Dr. M. Stephen James, professor of practical theology, to assume temporary administrative responsibilities, first as acting dean, then as acting president. He was finally recommended to the synod of 1953 as president of the seminary, though the administration had been essentially in his hands since Dr. Sizoo's resignation. A member of the faculty for ten years, Dr. James was highly esteemed in the Reformed Church, having served the First Church in Albany during the time when two congregations had been reunited and new educational facilities constructed.

In addition to financial problems, Dr. James inherited a number of other difficult situations that demanded immediate attention. A gap was left when Dr. Livingston Warnshuis, who had

167

been the primary architect of the school's financial well being, resigned as treasurer early in 1953. Dr. Beardslee, who had reached the mandatory retirement age in 1949 had, at the seminary's invitation, continued to be responsible for instruction in the New Testament department. In 1953, however, he no longer felt able to carry the full load, and Dr. Vernon Kooy, a graduate of Western Seminary, Princeton, and Union, was invited to become a lector to supplement Dr. Beardslee's teaching and ultimately to take over the department.

The most glaring problem, however, was the $150,000 Capital Fund Drive which had been authorized several years earlier. Virtually nothing had been done about it, although the deteriorating situation of some of the buildings required drastic atten-

M. Stephen James

tion. Dr. James's hard work had led to the increase of contributions from the churches to $47,000, but this just kept the budget in balance, with nothing extra for capital improvements. The seminary simply had to address itself to raising the $150,000 which had been authorized.

By 1954 enough money had been raised to enable the administration to do some planning. Since Dr. Hoffman would be retiring in 1956, it was proposed that his home at 27 Seminary Place, one of the most deteriorated of the seminary buildings, be demolished and in its place a new building be erected which would contain three faculty apartments and a guest room. The basic concept was approved, but no work was to be done until at least seventy-five percent of the funds needed were in hand from the money raised in the special drive.

In his report in 1954, which marked the completion of the first year of his presidency, Dr. James pointed out the opportunities which the seminary had "in its location at the heart of a rapidly growing State University." Specifically, he called for cooperation with the Rutgers Graduate School of Education for the development of degrees in the field of religious education. He also indicated an interest in the future development of a Protestant center for Rutgers, to be located on the seminary campus, quite possibly in a new building to be constructed on the site of 1 Seminary Place. While nothing ever came of either of these suggestions, it is worth noting that an awareness of the possibilities of closer cooperation with Rutgers University marked the beginning of the James administration.

Under the leadership of the then-acting-president's wife late in 1952, the women of the church were organized first into a Women's Committee and then a Women's Auxiliary to help with the desperate situation of furnishings in the dormitory rooms in Hertzog Hall and the more general needs of student comfort. Founded for this specific task, the auxiliary has continued over the years to be a tremendous help to the administration in looking after student housing and the general physical welfare of the campus.

Dr. Kooy's name was submitted to the synod of 1955 as Dr. Beardslee's successor to the New Testament chair. Two other faculty changes came in the following year when Dr. Milton Hoffman reached the mandatory retirement age, and Dr. Herbert Van Wyk resigned his office to return to the parish ministry. To replace Dr. Hoffman in the chair of church history, Dr. Wallace Jamison of the Department of History in Westminster College, New Wilmington, Pennsylvania, was secured as an adjunct professor.

A graduate of Westminster, Princeton Seminary, and Edinburgh, Dr. Jamison had served as a chaplain in the United States Navy as well as in several posts in the then United Presbyterian Church. Later in 1956 the Rev. Peter VandenBerge came to the seminary as lector in Christian education.

With Dr. Hoffman's retirement, the house at 27 Seminary Place was vacated. The fact that the Capital Fund Drive had by now yielded $115,000, made possible the demolition of the old building and the construction of the new one which replaced it. The plans which were finally adopted were somewhat more modest than those originally proposed. A building containing two faculty apartments of seven rooms each was constructed on the site and was ready for occupancy by 1957.

The year 1957 also brought another addition to the seminary's property through the reversion of Dr. Raven's home on Bishop Place to seminary ownership. The seminary now had a fine additional faculty residence. Dr. James soon designated it as the "President's House," and both he and his successor lived there.

Dr. Jamison was elected to the chair of church history by the General Synod in 1957 and in that same fall the now Mrs. Margaret Wilson resigned her post as librarian of Gardner Sage after nearly thirty years of service. Mr. VandenBerge gave up his teaching in Christian education, worked with Mrs. Wilson for a time while studying library science, and in October became her successor. Ever since becoming president, Dr. James had used supplementary help in the various aspects of the Department of Practical Theology. By 1957, he found that efforts to continue teaching while carrying his administrative burdens were impossible. The Rev. James Eelman, pastor of the Bethel Reformed Church in Passaic, New Jersey, was therefore invited to join the staff as lector in practical theology and began his duties that fall.

A year later Dr. James asked to be relieved of all teaching duties, resigning his chair of practical theology. Since he had only one year remaining before mandatory retirement, he wanted to devote that time fully to administration so that he might leave the school in the best possible situation. Mr. Eelman was recommended to the General Synod of 1958 and elected as professor of practical theology.

Dr. James's retirement came a year later. During his time as president New Brunswick Seminary had been strengthened in just about every way. Student enrollment had steadily increased to the point that it was now nearing seventy. Annual contributions from congregations had shown a continual increase, from $44,000 to $87,000, during his term of office. The budget had been balanced every year during his administration. A new faculty residence had been constructed and plans were underway for extensive repairs to Gardner Sage Library.

The seminary's 175th anniversary was celebrated at the close of Dr. James's administration. Although some local events were held, the celebration was designed as the 175th Anniversary of Theological Education in the Reformed Church in America, and the major event was a special service held in connection with the meeting of General Synod. The speaker was Dr. James I. McCord, newly-elected president of Princeton Seminary, whose topic was "The Idea of a Reformed Seminary."

In connection with the anniversary, Dr. James proposed the creation of the John Henry Livingston Chair of Theology, to be held by the presidents of New Brunswick Seminary during their terms of office. Pointing out that there was no worthy memorial to the seminary's first professor, he urged the creation of this chair to provide that much-needed remembrance. General Synod accepted the idea and, in accepting Dr. James's resignation, named him John Henry Livingston Professor Emeritus.

The same synod which accepted Dr. James's resignation elected Dr. Justin W. Vander Kolk as president of New Brunswick Seminary and named him the first John Henry Livingston Professor. Dr. Vander Kolk was certainly no stranger to the New Brunswick scene having served on the faculty for twelve years before becoming president. Because he was so popular as a teacher and so highly respected in the denomination, Dr. Vander Kolk's election was widely hailed. Everyone was sure that under his leadership the gains that had been made during the James administration would be consolidated and the seminary led to new heights of achievement.

Since Mr. VandenBerge had given up teaching Christian education to become librarian, the Rev. Roger Juckett, a Reformed Church pastor, was asked to come to Holy Hill to be a lector in that department, as well as to direct the whole area of field work. Theological education in a contextual situation had become an increasing part of seminary curricula in America generally since the Second World War and was an area in which New Brunswick had been lagging. Mr. Juckett's addition to the faculty, with responsibilities in both Christian education and field work, was a recognition of this deficiency and an attempt to remedy it.

Dr. Vander Kolk's administration began brightly. Student enrollment was at a record of sixty-nine; the financial picture was better than it had been in many years. Money for capital improvements made it possible to give major attention to the problems of Gardner Sage Library. A new heating system was installed in the fall of 1959, the roof underwent major repairs, and a cement floor was laid in the basement.

An unexpected shadow fell across the new administration on December 23, 1959, with the sudden death of Dr. Hugh MacLean. The disturbance that had surrounded his inaugural had long since been forgotten, and Dr. MacLean had become a highly regarded member of the faculty, widely esteemed for his abilities as a teacher as well as a helpful presence on the campus. During most of Dr. James's administration, as well as Dr. Vander Kolk's, MacLean had served as academic dean, relieving the presidents of a number of responsibilities in the area of academic affairs. His death came as a shock to the entire seminary community and left a void which it would be difficult to fill.

Relationships between New Brunswick and Western seminaries had become more distant in recent years so that there was widespread concern in the Reformed Church about their separateness. In his report on the State of Religion to the synod of 1960, retiring President Dr. Howard Hageman made two recommendations which were to affect the future of both schools. The first which won ready acceptance concerned regular meetings of the two faculties.

> Nothing is more essential to our unity as a denomination than our Theological Professors. It is our shame as a Reformed Church that we have never made it possible for them to meet together but have boxed them in their two respective situations. I therefore recommend that plans be made to convene all of our Theological Professors at the General Synod in 1961.[1]

A convocation of the two faculties was held in 1961 and for several years after that. Dr. Hageman's second suggestion was somewhat more tentative and was recommended for further study.

> Should we not consider the creation of one Board of Theological Education which, in terms of faculty and curriculum, would operate both seminaries in the name of the General Synod? Local needs could be cared for by committees but the central questions would be the responsibility of the entire Church.[2]

While neither proposal meant much at the time, except for the convening of faculty convocations, they were in a sense the beginning of significant future developments.

The year 1960 also saw the election of Dr. Gerrit Vander Lugt, former president of Central College, as professor of theology. Dr. James had learned the impossibility of combining administrative duties with full teaching responsibilities and, much as he loved

the classroom, Dr. Vander Kolk saw the wisdom in the example
of his predecessor and stepped down from his professorial chair.
Dr. Virgil M. Rogers of the faculty of Princeton Seminary was
invited to New Brunswick as lector in Old Testament studies, to
fill the vacancy created by Dr. MacLean's death. In 1961 he was
elected to the chair by General Synod.

One of the things which Dr. Vander Kolk learned of early in
his administration was the need for overall campus planning. A
second duplex house for faculty residences was built in 1961 along
the College Avenue side of the campus, with moneys borrowed
from unrestricted funds. One of the major needs of the school,
however, was for apartments for married students. The accommodations provided in Hertzog Hall and in other houses owned
by the seminary simply were inadequate. Apartments available
in the city of New Brunswick were prohibitively expensive. The
administration believed that this lack of facilities for married students constituted a real hindrance to efforts in recruitment.

Administrative offices in Hertzog Hall were also inadequate,
while the classroom space in Suydam Hall left much to be de-
sired. A new building which would combine classrooms and administrative offices on the site of Suydam Hall would meet a great
need in the seminary's life. Dreaming still further, one could
easily envision the need for a separate new chapel. Lovely as
Worcester Chapel on the second floor of Hertzog Hall was, it was
too small for any purpose except daily worship. The seminary
had no place for visiting lecturers, larger alumni gatherings, and
public assemblies.

During the year 1960 a special Planning and Development
Committee of the board studied all of the needs for future building. It rejected any idea of moving New Brunswick to another
site or of combining it with Western Seminary and concentrated
on the need for adequate facilities on Holy Hill. Its estimate for
the new buildings mentioned above, as well as a number of mis-
cellaneous items, came to a total of $1,250,000. While the need
for an additional $1,250,000 for the Endowment Fund was rec-
ognized, it was decided that the sum should be sought from

individuals, corporations, and foundations. The money for capital improvements on the campus should be raised from individual congregations.

Faced with the challenge of raising such a large sum of money for the physical renovation of New Brunswick Seminary, the congregations of the three eastern synods responded handsomely. In each of the three synods New Brunswick's cause was combined with those of local situations, with the result that in June of 1963 President Vander Kolk could report that a total of $1,356,000 had been pledged for capital improvements at the seminary. On the strength of moneys already received against those pledges, work was immediately begun on what everyone agreed was the primary need, a new apartment building for married students.

While Dr. Kooy was on sabbatical during the academic year of 1962-3, Dr. E. Earle Ellis was secured to take his place and his services were then retained as an additional member of the biblical department.

After such outstanding success in raising funds for the rebuilding of the campus, Dr. Vander Kolk offered his resignation as president on August 31, 1963, after an administration of only four years. Having brought the financial campaign to a successful con-- clusion, he had little appetite for all of the details that would be involved in planning and constructing the new buildings. Teaching was Vander Kolk's first love and he longed for a situation in which he could devote himself to teaching, as well as to study and writing. The board accepted his resignation with great reluctance and elected Dr. Jamison, professor of church history and dean of the seminary, as the new president.

Dr. Jamison had some vacancies to fill in the faculty. The Department of Christian Education and Field Work had been vacant ever since Mr. Juckett had been involved in a serious automobile accident which necessitated his resignation. Various temporary appointments had proved unsatisfactory. In the fall of 1963 the Rev. Charles Wissink, pastor of the Reformed Church in Clifton, New Jersey, who had been doing some lecturing at the seminary, was invited to occupy the vacant post. Dr. John W. Beardslee III of Central College was invited to become lector in church history to fill the vacancy created by Dr. Jamison's elevation to the presidency; in 1965 Beardslee was elected to the chair by the General Synod.

The real problem faced by Dr. Jamison was how to spend the money raised by the special drive. Everyone had agreed as to the necessity of the new apartment house for married students, which was opened in the fall of 1964 as Scudder Hall (named for the missionary family with which New Brunswick Seminary had been so closely associated), but what about the rest of the buildings which had been proposed in the plan of 1961? That plan had called for a new classroom and administration building, a new chapel, and, after some major renovations, the continued use of Hertzog Hall as a dormitory for single students. Rising costs over the estimates made in 1961 called for another look at the plan and possible alterations in it.

There was also a second factor that seemed to call for some hesitation in carrying out the plans of 1961. Ever since the be-

Scudder Hall

ginning of the decade there had been a growing number of voices in the Reformed Church which questioned the advisability of a small denomination's continuing to maintain two theological seminaries. It was not merely a question of the costs involved; in an age of steadily increasing specialization, there was the additional problem of having a larger faculty whose members would be free to teach in their specialized areas.

Both New Brunswick and Western had faculties consisting generally of one man per department. Occasionally, as in the case of the biblical department at New Brunswick, there were three people instead of two, and various adjuncts were brought into both schools to help supplement the curriculum. This did not, however, remove the fact that each professor had to be a generalist, simply unable to devote the time to the specialization that contemporary theological education was demanding. In view of the large specialized faculties in schools like Princeton or Union, was not the Reformed Church system condemning its students to a second rate training? If the additional $1,250,000 endowment had been raised for New Brunswick, as had been proposed in 1961, it would have helped to solve this problem, but that proposal had been shelved and never heard of again.

If it were possible to combine the two schools and locate them as a single institution in a neutral setting somewhere between New Brunswick, New Jersey, and Holland, Michigan, much of the difficulty could be overcome. The new school would have a faculty double the size of that in either of the two existing institutions, plus a greatly expanded library. Such a school could probably take its place with the leading theological seminaries in the country. As for the costs involved, the sale of the New Brunswick site to Rutgers University, then in the process of rapid expansion, and of the Holland site to Hope College would largely cover them.

With such discussions very much in the forefront of Reformed Church thinking, it seemed imprudent to go forward with any building plans at New Brunswick. The Permanent Committee on Theological Education, the synod's new agency for dealing with the seminaries, reported to the synod of 1965 that while it had considered the possible merger of the two schools, its final judgment was that their continuation as two institutions was in the best interest of the denomination. At the same time, however, it called for continuation toward the goal of more effective unification and coordination of theological education in the Reformed Church.

Taking this as a signal that an institution on Holy Hill in New Brunswick had some kind of a future, the board voted in the spring of 1966 to demolish both Suydam and Hertzog halls and replace them with a new all-purpose building. The decision to demolish Hertzog was based on an architect's report that its renovation would cost at least twice as much as its replacement. That verdict was called into question by a number of alumni, but the plan went forward and by the summer of 1966 both Suydam and Hertzog had been destroyed.[3]

This meant that the academic year 1966-7 was a time of great upheaval at New Brunswick. The destruction of both buildings took away classrooms, chapel, administrative offices, and dormitory rooms for single students. Adjustments were made in the best possible manner. Classes were held in the library, chapel in the living room of 3 Seminary Place, the home formerly occupied by Dr. and Mrs. Kooy, and some accommodations for single students were found upstairs in the same home. All in all, it was a trying year, especially when to the dislocations on campus there was added the rising commotion in the church caused by the elimination of Hertzog Hall.

Apparently the administration and board were sensitive to some of these criticisms of what had been done. Reporting to the General Synod of 1967, the actions were defended on the ground that these were necessary replacements and that the money had already been raised for them in the Capital Fund Drive. Zwemer Hall, as the new facility was named, was dedicated on October 2, 1967. Named for Samuel Zwemer, the New Brunswick graduate who had been the pioneer missionary to Arabia, the new building was a simple, functional one accommodating cafeteria, class-rooms, and administrative offices.

The most striking feature of Zwemer Hall was the chapel which crowned Holy Hill at the center of the new building. The architectural intention was to provide a modern counterpart to Old Queens on the Rutgers hill two blocks away. With little sensitivity to the history of the institution, no provision was made for either the Hertzog bell or the Dutch carillon which were put into storage. It was apparently the thought of the administration that a strikingly new and different style of building would not only identify the school with the future but would also attract new students to an enrollment which had already fallen to forty.

The construction of Zwemer Hall was the last action of the old Board of Superintendents which passed out of existence in 1967. What had been a lengthy discussion in the church terminated that year in the creation of a single Board of Theological Education charged with responsibility for the operation of the two schools. Although it was obviously not yet ready to spell out any

Zwemer Hall

details, the new board saw its task as unifying theological education in the Reformed Church in America. Having unified the board, the next step was seen in a unification of the faculty at a date in the near future.

In the meantime, there were changes in the New Brunswick faculty. Dr. Vander Lugt, having reached the mandatory retirement age, resigned his position as professor of theology while Professor Eelman also resigned the chair of practical theology to return to the parish ministry. Later in the year Mr. VandenBerge resigned as librarian to accept a similar position with Colgate-Rochester Seminary.

In 1967 the faculty recommended two changes in academic procedure which were approved by the board. With faculty permission seminary students were to be permitted to take courses in the graduate departments of Rutgers University which would be credited as electives in the New Brunswick curriculum. The three-term schedule was also abandoned and the old semester plan revived so that a closer correspondence between New Brunswick and Rutgers course offerings might be possible.

To replace the vacancies in the faculty, the Rev. D. LeRoy Englehardt came as librarian, the Rev. Paul Fries was invited to be lector in systematic theology, and the Rev. Harold Miner in practical theology. Mr. Miner was a minister in the Southern Presbyterian Church, which at that time was in serious union negotiations with the Reformed Church in America. The choice of Miner for the position at New Brunswick indicated the growing relationship between the two denominations.

The new Board of Theological Education had taken seriously its mandate to unify theological education in the Reformed Church and had secured the help of Dr. Gordon Kaufman of Harvard Divinity School as its consultant. As a preliminary step it recommended in 1968 that New Brunswick be authorized, in cooperation with Rutgers, to offer the masters degree in theology, which it described as a "lay degree in theology . . . consistent with the increasing emphasis on diversity and cooperation in theological education."

It was in its report to the synod of 1969, meeting in New Brunswick, that the direction in which the new board was moving became clearer. The synod meeting that year was a somewhat emotional one: James Foreman conducted his demonstration asking the Reformed Church for idemnification and, out of frustration over the defeat of union with the Southern Presbyterian Church, a committee was appointed to study the possibility of dividing the Reformed Church into two separate churches. In such an emotionally charged atmosphere it is possible that the board's report did not get a careful hearing, but its proposals were clearly spelled out.

In the board's thinking, the unification of theological education meant that, in addition to a single board, both institutions would have a single president. The board therefore recommended that Dr. Jamison be relieved of his duties as president of New Brunswick Seminary and be given a year's sabbatical leave as a professor of theology. In the future, presidents were not to occupy the John Henry Livingston chair, to avoid any suggestion that they had tenure of office. To replace Dr. Jamison the board recommended the election of Dr. Herman Ridder, the president of Western Seminary, as president of both schools.

Recognizing that a common president would mean a strong administrator resident in each school, the board indicated that it was in negotiation with someone to serve as dean of New Brunswick Seminary under President Ridder, but that the negotiations were not yet complete. That someone turned out to be Dr. Norman Thomas, pastor of the First Church in Albany, New York, who was unable to resume his new duties before January of 1970.

Although the board was not yet ready with its full plan for the unification of theological education in the Reformed Church, it indicated that what it was working on was what it called a "bi-level two site" program, part of which would be taken at New Brunswick and part at Western. The first section would be called Christian Identity and the second the Professional Ministry. This new program would not be merely combining two existing curricula into one, but "a program of ministerial training which is more adequate for the changing modern world and more continuous with the actual work of the ministry in it." Some experiments in these new directions were already taking place in New Brunswick, but a total revision of the curriculum in both schools would await the final presentation of the board's plan in 1970.

As a small footnote to all of these great new visions, the board authorized the purchase of a multiple-dwelling building in Hiram Street in New Brunswick to provide additional housing units. The expected new program would involve the presence of more students on the New Brunswick campus than its facilities could accommodate, and the Hiram Street unit would afford direct contact with the problems and demands of inner-city life.

Standing on the threshold of 1970, New Brunswick Seminary, now a school of only thirty-six students, looked forward to the beginning of a whole new chapter in its 185-year-old history. It was to be continued but no longer as an independent school. Instead it was to be part of an overall design for one program of theological education in the Reformed Church in America. Those who had designed the new program were aware of the dangers involved but even more convinced of its great new possibilities.

> The Board hopes and prays that we will trust each other sufficiently to at least allow this unified program a chance to prove its value. It believes that the program contains the vital bridge to understanding, East and West, which is necessary if we are to be a church. That it contains risks and is partially a dream, we admit. But with the opportunity we have to *dare* to more adequately meet the needs of the church and through it the needs of this revolutionary world, we cannot but seize the opportunity and do so with dispatch.[4]

XII

Brave New Experiment

The Board of Theological Education spent a busy 1969 getting its proposals ready for the synod of 1970. The two seminaries had one board and one administration; what remained to be done was to unite them in a single program of theological training.

These proposals were presented to the synod and approved in June of 1970, though not without some important modification. The essence of the program was a combined education, with the first two years spent at New Brunswick and the second two years at Western. It was understood that some students might be able to complete the final part of the program in less than two years, while some might require more. The first level at New Brunswick was described as follows.

> The first level of this program which has as its purpose to teach men to live and act in the world with theological understanding will be offered at the New Brunswick site. The concern at this level is not primarily that of the production of a professional minister but rather the preparation of a Christian person.[1]

When a student moved to Western Seminary for the second level, he would there be equipped with the professional skills necessary for ministry. If the New Brunswick level could be described as concerned with the production of a Christian person, the Western level had as its object the production of a Christian minister. In the original proposal the new program was to become operative in the fall of 1970 and mandatory in 1972. No new admissions to the traditional three-year program were to be received in either school after the fall of 1971.

To supplement the faculty at New Brunswick for its new task,

Professor Hugh Koops was moved from the faculty at Western. Since his special field was ethics, a department not represented at New Brunswick and a critical one for the new program, Professor Koops presence was very important. It was also indicated that the master in Christian education program would by 1971 be consolidated on the New Brunswick campus in cooperation with the Rutgers School of Education.

Since there were eight overtures before the General Synod, all of them from classes in the Midwest and all of them opposing the new program to one degree or another, the board modified its own report at one significant point. It removed the 1971 cut-off date for enrollment in the traditional three-year program, promising to continue it for as long as it was necessary. At the same time, the board expressed its confidence that the excellence of the new program would be such that any demand for the continuance of the traditional three-year program at a single site would soon disappear. Indeed enrollment figures in the fall of 1970 seemed to justify the prediction. A record number of students applied, most of them for the new program.

The large increase in the number of students at New Brunswick because of the new program made for an acute housing problem. That, for single students, was solved by taking 25 Seminary Place, the former home of Dr. Jamison, as a dormitory for single students, as had been done earlier with the former home of Dr. Kooy at 3 Seminary Place. The problem of apartments for married students posed more difficulties. The project in Hiram Street had run into considerable opposition from the Hispanic community and the negotiations necessary to try to resolve these problems meant that there was no way in which they could be ready by the fall of 1970. A block of apartments was rented in a development across the Raritan and the cost of rentals there was subsidized with the hope that this would be only a temporary expedient.

If the first year was any indication of the future of the Bi-Level Multi-Site program, it seemed destined for great success. Not only was enrollment at an all-time high, but much of it was in

the new program for which a number of new students displayed
great enthusiasm. The experiment was greeted by many outside
observers in the field of theological education as one worth
watching.

By the synod of 1971, however, some of the euphoria of the
first year had begun to dissipate. The most serious blow which
the new program suffered in May of that year was the resignation
of President Herman Ridder to return to the parish ministry. He
had been so instrumental not only in designing the program but
in representing it to the church that his resignation was universally recognized as a serious loss. A second problem was that the
church had not responded to the new program with any degree
of financial enthusiasm; giving to the cause of theological education had dropped noticeably to the extent that the proposed budget for the coming year had to be reduced drastically.

Dr. Lester Kuyper of the Western faculty was asked to serve
as interim president of the two schools and the hope was expressed that a successor to Dr. Ridder could be found by the end
of 1971.

The Hiram Street property had run into so much community
opposition, including numerous cases of arson, that it was decided
to sell the property and give up the whole experiment. Married
students who could not be accommodated in Scudder Hall were
to be accommodated in various apartments in New Brunswick,
but the financial situation did not permit any continuance of the
policy of subsidization which had been adopted a year earlier.

The year 1971 did bring one significant change which was taking place in American theological education generally. For years
there had been unhappiness over the fact that a graduate program
lasting three years should be rewarded with nothing but a second
bachelor's degree. The Association of Theological Schools had
recommended to its members that they should take whatever
steps were necessary to change the name of the degree from
bachelor of divinity to master of divinity. New Brunswick and
Western accepted the change, and the class of 1971 was the first
to receive the new degree.

By 1972 it was apparent that a number of shadows were beginning to fall across the Bi-Level Multi-Site program which had
begun with such enthusiasm. In the opening of its report to the
synod that year the board listed the mounting problems which
it was facing:

> The adoption of a record high budget for 1972-73, increased financial
> support for theological education, mounting deficits, completion of
> the first level of the new unified BLMS program by more than a
> dozen students, declining enrollments in that program but [in-
> creased] enrollments in the three year program, [and] failure to find
> a permanent president. . . .[2]

Whatever may have been the case in other parts of the church,
it was clear that the congregations in the eastern synods were not
giving the program generous financial support. Contributions from
those synods to theological education had not increased since the
unification of the two schools, although the budget, especially at
New Brunswick, had increased enormously.

During the spring of 1972 the board had also been involved in
a bruising battle over the presidency. By a very close vote that
office had been offered to the Rev. Arie Brouwer with the understanding that while accepting it he could retain his office as
General Secretary of the General Program Council of the Reformed Church in America. After extensive visits to the seminaries, as well as with Reformed Church leaders, Mr. Brouwer
concluded that such a combination of offices was not acceptable
in the Reformed Church and declined the offer.

Brouwer's refusal meant that so far as leadership was concerned, the board was exactly where it had been. It also meant
that the wide discussion which had taken place in the church
about the possibility of combining the presidency of the seminaries with the office of secretary of the General Program Council
had led to a growing distrust of the Board of Theological Education. To many it seemed that the drive for unification and cen-
tralization had in this case gone too far. Questions which had not

previously been asked now began to be raised about the whole new program of theological education.

Students were apparently beginning to ask questions, too. At both New Brunswick and Western seminaries the number of those enrolling for the joint program had begun to decline, while the number seeking admission to the traditional three-year program continued to increase. This placed a heavy burden on the faculty of Western Seminary which virtually had to maintain two programs, one for the second level of the joint program as well as one for the three-year students. The problem was less pressing for the faculty at New Brunswick where it was possible to combine much of the first level program with that of the first two years of the traditional curriculum.

At the 1972 fall meeting of the board it was decided to abandon the search for a single president for both schools. There had been support for a single presidency, although for some that contained the proviso that the president reside at "their" school. Others had concluded that a president for each institution was inevitable. When representatives of each school were able to achieve a high degree of unanimity on a candidate of their choice, it was decided that each institution should once again have its own president. At the meeting of January, 1973, it was decided that the unified budget, which had been tried for several years, was to be replaced with separate financial programs for each school. The two candidates were presented to the board—John Hesselink for the presidency of Western Seminary and Howard Hageman for that of New Brunswick. Each president was offered a term of five years. The General Synod in June of that year confirmed the board's action.

At the same time that the decision was reached to secure two presidents, the board reaffirmed its commitment to a unified board and to the Bi-Level Multi-Site program. It was felt that the basic concept which had been worked out over the years should remain and that the greater administrative efficiency gained by having two presidents should help strengthen it. In point of fact, the concept of a unified Board of Theological Education did last, but the Bi-Level Multi-Site program became a matter of history in just a few years.

It is perhaps too soon after the event to assess the lasting effects of the experiment on New Brunswick Seminary, but a few observations can certainly be made. Despite the large increase in numbers during the first year or so of enthusiasm, as student commitment to the program began to wane, the enrollment at New Brunswick was no larger than it had been in the closing years of the Jamison administration. The diminished interest in the combined program was the result of falling income, generally experienced by educational institutions at this time, which resulted in the inability of the board to support Bi-Level Multi-Site students to the degree they felt they had been promised. Because of the economic situation, the job market for student wives was very different in Holland from what it was in New Brunswick. It was the economy which impaired an otherwise carefully-thought-out program.

The financial resources with which the seminary had to face the future were considerably diminished. The new program had added large amounts to the seminary's budget. It had to assume the salaries for a dean and an additional faculty member, half the salary for a president, and half the salary for a development officer. In addition there was the money lost on the Hiram Street project, though much of that was retrieved through the sale of the property.

For all these additional expenses there was no additional income. The expected increase in support from congregations never became a reality. The unified budget made no provision for the increased expenses at New Brunswick. The result was that an institution which had paid its own way for many years was forced to draw out almost all of its capital reserves to meet its new expenses. The institution which was returned to its own control in 1973 was financially much weaker than it had been before the experiment began.

Worst of all, as it began to be clear that the Bi-Level Multi-Site program was not likely to succeed, New Brunswick Seminary

faced a problem in morale. An increasing number of voices in the
Reformed Church raised the old question about the need for two
seminaries. Since Western was obviously the healthier of the two
schools, why not sell out New Brunswick and combine forces
there? Even though a special committee of the synod appointed
to study the question of locations recommended the maintenance
of the two schools for the immediate present, questions about the
continued need for New Brunswick were not put to rest.

That kind of uncertainty about the future was demoralizing to
the faculty who did not know how long their jobs at New Brunswick might continue, to the student body who could not be sure
that they would graduate from the same school which they had
entered, and to congregations which were reluctant to contribute
to what many were sure was a dying cause. A school which celebrated its 189th anniversary in the fall of 1973 was not at all
certain it would survive to celebrate its 200th birthday in 1984.

Installation service for Howard G. Hageman, 1973

It was the wish of President Hageman to end his story with his appointment to the presidency. The Bicentennial Committee on Publications felt it would be impossible to write a history of the first two centuries of New Brunswick without including the important events and significant changes in both faculty, curriculum, and outreach of the seminary during Dr. Hageman's presidency.

The publications committee of the seminary solicited the services of the Rev. Benjamin Alicea who was appointed in 1978 to serve as instructor in church history and as associate director of the Urban Theological Center Program. Presently, Mr. Alicea serves as dean of the Evening Theological Education Program and as assistant professor of church history.

We are grateful to Mr. Alicea for providing that necessary history which Dr. Hageman in his modesty left to another to recount.

XIII

New Vision For a New Day

During the seventies and early eighties New Brunswick Seminary took bold steps to carry out its historic mission in theological education. Beginning with the appointment of Dr. Hageman as president, the seminary began creating a new identity and focus. New Brunswick inaugurated the urban program, a truly innovative model in adult theological education. Faculty and administrative appointments were made for urban ministry. Relationships with neighboring educational institutions were strengthened, and doors were opened to students from abroad. As the institution approached its bicentennial, it changed its approach to accommodate a new urban reality.

Howard Hageman came to New Brunswick's helm at a difficult time in the institution's history. He was, however, well prepared for the task before him. For twenty-eight years he had served as pastor of the North Reformed Church in downtown Newark, New Jersey. He had taught homiletics and liturgics at the seminary and was well known throughout the Reformed Church in America as an outstanding preacher, author of such widely read books as *Lily Among the Thorns*, *Pulpit and Table*, and *Predestination*, and a former president of General Synod (1959-60). Dr. Hageman was an alumnus of Harvard University, 1942, and New Brunswick Seminary, 1945. He had received honorary doctorates from Central College (1957), Hope College (1975), Ursinus College (1975), and Knox College, Toronto (1977). The announcement of Dr. Hageman's appointment was envisioned as a significant step toward the revitalization of Holy Hill.

The philosophy of ministry and education Dr. Hageman brought

to his new responsibilities as president was articulated in his inaugural address, entitled "A Funny Thing Happened on the Way
to New Brunswick" and delivered on October 1, 1973, at the
First Reformed Church in New Brunswick, New Jersey.[1] His
address reflected a clear understanding of the objectives the seminary needed to pursue, although he confessed he was unclear
about the best means to achieve them. Although he had not
served previously in an academic administrative position, his
twenty-eight years of pastoral experience in an urban parish had
prepared him uniquely for the task. In the conclusion of his address Dr. Hageman stated: "If ever there was a day in which we
could think of theological education as a cloistered experience of
three detached years, that day has passed."

During Dr. Hageman's tenure as president, the seminary has
moved beyond traditional conceptions of theological education
and has discovered much about itself, its surroundings, and its
mission to the church of Jesus Christ. It has begun to look beyond
the banks of the Raritan River, to the great metropolitan area

Howard G. Hageman

and its burgeoning pluralistic communities. New Brunswick Seminary has stepped forward to serve new students from racial and ethnic minority groups from many denominations, along with its traditional RCA constituency.

The dramatic change in the population of students at the seminary can best be illustrated by comparing the student bodies of 1973 and 1983.[2] In 1973, there were 43 students enrolled, all white males, averaging 24 years of age. Ninety-eight percent were master of divinity students, and 84 percent were Reformed Church candidates, with 88 percent residing on Holy Hill. The contrast in 1983 is remarkable. There were 110 students enrolled, 64 percent male and 61 percent white, averaging 37 years of age. The percentage of master of divinity students declined from 98 percent to 81.8 percent, with 35.4 percent of the entire enrollment preparing for Reformed Church ministry (46.8 percent on the New Brunswick campus). Only 27 percent of the students were now residing on campus. The reasons for this dramatic change in the composition and nature of the student body are explained in part by developments within the Reformed Church, but the primary reason is the impact of the New York/Urban Program.

In 1974, the General Synod, at the request of the Reformed Church Minority councils, recommended that the Reformed Church seminaries "present suggestions and a progress report . . . as to how the training of ethnic minority students could be implemented in our seminaries. . . ."[3] Prior to the 1974 General Synod, informal conversations between the seminary administration and representatives of the councils were held to explore ways of mutual assistance and recruitment of students. There was an openness and a desire to provide theological training for minority candidates at New Brunswick Seminary, but concern was expressed by the councils that New Brunswick was not equipped to provide appropriate theological education for ministry among racial/ethnic groups.

This concern expressed by the minority councils was not without basis. What the faculty knew about the minority church was limited. However, the reality of the racial and ethnic composition of the Northeast and the need for larger enrollment led the faculty to acquaint itself more thoroughly with the rudiments of the minority church experience. This learning process, gradual and difficult at times, was vital to the institution in its search for a significant place and identity as an urban and Reformed theological training center.

The genesis of the urban program can be traced to an informal and unexpected conversation in Hertzog Hall following a Lenten service. During Lent, guest preachers are often invited to lead the seminary's weekly Wednesday night worship service. However, on a Wednesday night during Lent in 1975, the seminary benefited from more than a sermon from its guest. During the coffee hour after worship, the guest preacher, the Rev. Dr. George W. (Bill) Webber, president of New York Theological Seminary (NYTS) in New York City, asked Dr. Hageman if New Brunswick Seminary was interested in providing instruction for a number of adults in New York City who felt a call to the Christian ministry and needed the master of divinity degree for ordination, but who, for a number of reasons, were unable to attend an accredited seminary on the customary full-time basis. NYTS was not accredited to offer the master of divinity degree and was seeking to establish a partnership with a local seminary which would grant the degree.

In the fall of 1975, New Brunswick and New York seminaries entered into an agreement to share teaching resources and facilities and to begin an experimental part-time evening master of divinity program in New York City. A genuine partnership developed in which the faculties of both seminaries, students and staffs, collaborated to provide training for ministry for leaders in this metropolitan area. The traditional three-year residential program was redesigned into a four-year evening program in New York, with intensive summer courses on the New Brunswick campus. Classes were held on Monday and Wednesday evenings at New York Seminary, a convenient mid-town Manhattan location, with New Brunswick faculty members commuting into the city. The student body was a racially-integrated, multicultural group of mature adults, both lay and clergy, representing many denominations. In this form the joint program flourished until 1982, when it was terminated by New York Seminary's decision to reinstate their master of divinity program.

New Brunswick Seminary was faced with the challenge of meeting its obligations to New York/Urban Program degree candidates who expected to complete the program with New Brunswick, yet the seminary no longer had a New York site. About the same time, a management consultant was engaged to meet with the Management Committee and faculty to set new objectives for the seminary. One of the results of these consultations was a consensus that the seminary should continue providing quality, relevant and accredited theological education for mature men and women in the greater metropolitan area.

The spring and summer of 1983 were anxiety-ridden as New Brunswick Seminary struggled to find a suitable way to continue its evening theological education program. A design team, composed of New Brunswick students, alumni, and faculty and board members was commissioned to explore possibilities for the continuation of an evening urban program. A geographic study of the student body and their transportation patterns revealed that Jamaica, Queens, was a centrally-located community for a large percentage of the student body. The Design Team in consultation with the Rev. John Englehardt, a member of the Board of Theological Education and pastor of the First Reformed Church of Jamaica, visited First Church as a possible site for the program. They also visited St. John's University, which was located near the church and housed an excellent theology department and library. The seminary discovered that the church was ideally located near public transportation, had ample parking facilities nearby, and was in the heart of a community typical of the kind for which the school was training students. In addition, the seminary was graciously received by the theological department and administration of St. John's University, which empathized with the predicament the seminary was facing and consented to assist New Brunswick Seminary become established in Queens.

Despite the difficulties and uncertainty caused by the disso-
lution of the joint program, New Brunswick emerged with new
hope and confidence. The students who enrolled in the new
program and the opportunities that it offered for training mature
men and women committed to urban ministry formed the basis
for this optimism. After seven years of sharing the responsibility
for urban theological education with another institution, New
Brunswick Seminary was called to assume full accountability for
the enterprise.

Another significant development in the seminary enrollment
during the last ten years which has altered the traditional composition of the student body is the enrollment of women students
in the master of divinity degree program. Since 1977, twenty-
two women have been awarded the divinity degree and three
women the master of arts in theology degree. The average number of female students enrolled annually in the seminary since
1976 was twenty-eight. The institution which was populated almost exclusively by men for so many years has attracted an increasing number of women candidates for the ministry.

Dr. Hageman inherited a staff thoroughly trained in the major
theological disciplines. The faculty has continued to grow in number, expanding from one professor/president at its beginning, to
a large and diversified faculty, especially during this era to serve
the urban theological education program. The first addition to
the faculty under the presidency of Dr. Hageman was the administrative and faculty appointment of the Rev. Benjamin Alicea
as Director of Urban Studies in June of 1978. Alicea was the
founder of the Seekers Campus Ministry in New York City and
a Puerto Rican Pentecostal minister who transferred to the Reformed Church in 1980. He brought a knowledge of city ministry
that was needed in administration and policy formation.

After the resignation of Dr. Fries, the Rev. Isaac C. Rotten-
berg taught theology for one year until the appointment of the
Rev. George Hunsinger as professor of theology in 1979. Hunsinger holds degrees from Stanford University and Harvard Divinity School and is a Ph.D candidate at Yale University. He is

the editor of *Karl Barth and Radical Politics* and has published numerous articles and reviews. Ordained by the United Presbyterian Church in 1981, he has been an active voice in the nuclear disarmament movement.

When Dr. Norman Thomas left the seminary to become pastor of the Community Church in Bayside, Queens, he was succeeded by the Rev. Frederick Mold who joined the administration of the seminary after a twenty-five-year career in parish ministry, twenty-one years of which he spent as pastor of the Reformed Church of Freehold, New Jersey. Since 1957 he has served as stated clerk and treasurer of the Classis of New Brunswick. A graduate of Muhlenberg College and New Brunswick Seminary, he has served on the Board of Theological Education and the Management Committee. Mr. Mold is presently vice president for administration and instructor in pastoral administration and Reformed Church, polity.

The significant increase in the black student population resulting from the urban program called attention to the need for a black faculty presence. The seminary responded with two significant appointments. The first black faculty appointment in the history of the seminary was that of the Rev. Wilbur Washington, alumnus of Rutgers and New Brunswick, and former professor/counselor at Central College. He was invited to spend a year (1980-81) as a visiting professor at New Brunswick. Washington accepted the invitation and subsequently was appointed assistant professor of practical theology (homiletics) and director of supervised ministry (formerly field education) in 1982. He was conferred an honorary doctorate by Central College in May of 1982. The Rev. Marvin McMickle was the second faculty appointment. Pastor of the St. Paul's Baptist Church, current president of the New Jersey Council of Churches, and a recent graduate of Princeton Theological Seminary, Dr. McMickle was named director of the Urban Theological Education Program (UTEC).

As the seminary enters its third century, anticipated changes in personnel will no doubt give new emphases both to administration and instruction. More than half the present faculty will have retired by the end of this decade,[4] thereby altering the composition and personality of the faculty.

For a relatively small seminary, New Brunswick has provided an exceptionally diverse range of educational opportunities for its students and alumni. It has entered a number of creative institutional relationships which have enriched the curriculum, provided new degree opportunities, and opened doors for study abroad. The institutions NBTS has teamed with include Rutgers University, Princeton Theological Seminary, the Graduate School of Drew University, and the Trinity Counseling Center.

One continuing institutional arrangement has involved Rutgers, the large state university which surrounds the New Brunswick campus. Rutgers has cooperated by permitting cross-registration in its graduate divisions and has teamed with New Brunswick Seminary faculty to offer a master of arts degree in church music, and joint degree programs which combine theological degrees with social work (M.S.W.), education (M.Ed.), and library science (M.L.S.). Master of arts students in particular have availed themselves of the Rutgers courses since they are required to complete a portion of their degree requirements at Rutgers or another approved university. Many seminary students and spouses have participated in seminars, lecture series, and other educational and social events scheduled at the university. The Demarest-Livingston lectureship series, sponsored with funds administered by General Synod, brought Rutgers professors to New Brunswick Seminary from 1975-78. In recent years several New Brunswick Seminary students have pursued doctoral studies at Rutgers. In addition, students have had access to the entire bibliographical collection of the state university, and Gardner Sage Library has become an affiliated member of the university library network. The opportunities for interaction at many levels with Rutgers has been a rewarding feature of seminary life.

Prior to Dr. Hageman's inauguration, acting president Dr. Lester Kuyper and Dean Thomas began the negotiations with Princeton Theological Seminary which led to the establishment of the Princeton doctor of ministry program, with the assistance of New Brunswick faculty. In 1979 the Board of Theological Education evaluated the participation of New Brunswick in the doctor of ministry program and agreed to continue providing one-quarter of the administration and instruction.

The newest joint venture between Princeton and New Brunswick seminaries was the establishment of a Clinical Pastoral Education (CPE) program located at Middlesex General University Hospital in New Brunswick, the new teaching hospital of the state university. There has been an obvious need for accredited CPE training in this area for years. Students from the two Reformed seminaries have had to commute to New York City or remote parts of New Jersey to receive CPE training. The new CPE program will serve four major functions: 1) provide accredited CPE to theological students and clergy; 2) provide seminars and continuing education opportunities for area clergy; 3) provide in-service programs for hospital staff and medical students; and 4) provide instruction for hospital ministry to theological students in programs less formal than accredited CPE. The Rev. John deVelder, who graduated from New Brunswick Seminary in 1968, is serving as director of the program.

Another recent development in joint programs with neighboring institutions involves a cooperative masters in theology degree (Th.M.) with the Trinity Counseling Service in Princeton, New Jersey. New Brunswick Seminary is a partner in the only program of this kind in New Jersey for working pastors who desire advanced clinical training in pastoral care and counseling.

A program of liturgical studies leading to the Ph.D. degree from the Graduate School of Drew University was begun in the fall of 1977. Dr. Hageman, Professor Horton Davies of Princeton University, and Dean Bard Thompson of Drew University were the charter members of an ecumenical faculty of liturgical scholars who sustain this program. Presently, several New Brunswick Seminary alumni are working in it on advanced degrees.

The historic Dutch city of Leiden, located about eighteen miles southwest of Amsterdam, has been the site of the summer seminars in theology since the idea was conceived and implemented by Dr. Fries. Beginning in 1974, the *zomercursus* has convened biannually, except for 1982. New Brunswick Seminary has co-operated with the theological faculty of Leiden University, and other organizations in the Hague, to make this educational opportunity possible. An average of thirty New Brunswick students have joined others at Leiden from around the world, especially the Third World, to explore how the Christian tradition relates to the contemporary world. These New Brunswick students who have participated in this summer experience have enjoyed enormously the rich learning experiences in and outside the classroom.

Cooperative relationships have not only brought New Brunswick Seminary students to other campuses, but international students have also traveled to New Brunswick. For example, several South African students have received theological training at the seminary. The first was the Rev. Elia Mashai Tema, an ordained pastor and leader in the Dutch Reformed Church in South Africa (black). He was introduced to New Brunswick by Dr. Hageman when he visited South Africa in 1974. Pastor Tema arrived at the seminary having had previous theological training at the Stofberg Theological College (Pietersburg) and Vrije Universiteit (Amsterdam). He was awarded a masters in theology (May of 1976) and returned home where he serves a church in Soweto, the largest black township of Johannesburg.

Two independent but related actions have made it possible for three South African students to be on the New Brunswick campus during the early eighties. The first was the recommendation of the Christian Action Commission to the General Synod of the Reformed Church[5] that the General Program Council and the Board of Theological Education establish a scholarship fund to facilitate the exchange of students between Reformed Church seminaries in the United States and Stellenbosch University and Stofberg Theological College in South Africa. After a year of study the synod decided "to invite, under the auspices of New Brunswick Theological Seminary, a Black or Colored student from South Africa to study at New Brunswick for a period of one year."[6]

Funding, however, was a major obstacle. How would the travel, tuition, and personal expenses of these South Africans be financed? The generosity and sensitivity of the United Reformed Church of Somerville, pastored by the Rev. Douglass W. Fromm, Jr. (M.Div., '67), provided the second step necessary to permit South African students to study at New Brunswick. In the winter of 1980 a significant portion of the Van Cleef Fund of United Church was designated to finance the educational expenses of a Third World student attending the seminary. The Van Cleef International Fellowship Program provided sufficient funds for a year's study and for travel costs as recommended by the faculty of the seminary. The student was to be an ordained clergyperson from the Third World and was to pursue masters studies, though not necessarily as a degree candidate. The student also was to be committed to return to his or her native land to make a contribution there. Thus far the fund has enabled three South African students to come to New Brunswick, to share in the seminary community, to receive a degree, and to return home. They are: Michael Mohamed (M.A., 1982), David Mogaly Matshitse (M.A., 1982) and Zachariah Ezeqiel Mokgoebo (M.A., 1983). Each has returned to continue in the struggle for justice and equality in southern Africa.

With the 200th anniversary of New Brunswick approaching, discussions were begun to explore a fitting commemoration of the event. For several years the need to refurbish and renovate the library had been discussed. The Management Committee decided to request permission from General Synod to launch a denomination-wide appeal for capital funds. The name given to this effort was the New Brunswick Commitment.

The appeal was made to congregations in the Reformed Church in America, alumni, faculty, friends, and foundations to support four specific projects estimated to cost $1,500,000. The first project was the restoration and rehabilitation of the Gardner Sage Library, calculated at a cost $1,250,000. The second project was the endowment of the Urban Theological Education Center Program. The rapid growth and importance of UTEC to the seminary required a wider financial base. The target amount for this need was $12,500, to be realized from a restricted endowment of $125,000. The third aspect of the commitment was the establishment of a fund for Supervised Ministries. Currently, the seminary was unable to place, with remuneration, all students who needed to fulfill their requirements for supervised ministry (formerly called field education). This endowment would be $375,000 and would yield an annual income of $37,500. The fourth project was the campus reorientation and upgrading. New access roads to the seminary and the absence of a main entrance to Zwemer Hall dictated the need for this project at a cost of $250,000. Zwemer Hall was renovated and the entrance to Bishop Place was opened.

On the eve of the bicentennial, additional costs have raised the total expenses of these projects to $2,435,000. The seminary has employed the Rev. Dr. Russell J. Redeker to follow up on the New Brunswick Commitment and to establish a development office for the seminary.

During the New Brunswick Commitment fund drive, the library was extensively renovated to restore its beauty, expand the capacity, and improve the work space. The alterations to Sage Library included functionally turning the library around 180 degrees and creating a new entrance permitting access for the disabled; restoration of the interior and exterior of the building; remodeling of the transept known as the Wessell's addition with air conditioning and humidity control for the archives, rare books room, and staff working areas; dropping the Van Pelt alcove to the basement and opening up the basement to daylight and a new outdoor patio area. These renovations were intended to modernize the facility while preserving its pristine beauty. The renovation, begun in January of 1982, was completed in April of 1983.

Only for one day did the construction at Gardner Sage come to a halt. The contractors took a day off because Sage would host royalty! New Brunswick Seminary and Sage Library were honored by a visit from the queen of the Netherlands, Her Majesty Queen Beatrix and her husband, His Royal Highness Prince Claus, on June 28, 1982. At the joint invitation of New Brunswick Seminary and the State University of New Jersey, the queen visited New Brunswick as part of a two-week tour of the United States.[7] The queen's day in New Brunswick[8] included the opening of an exhibition of rare books, pictures, and manuscripts from the library's collection called "The Dutch in Two Worlds: Treasures from the Sage Collection."

Gardner Sage Library is the most majestic building on the New Brunswick Seminary campus. Perhaps the most spectacular view on the campus may be found within the walls that house the extensive library collection and the archives of the denomination, under the care of the Commission on History and the Office of the Historical Services of the Reformed Church. A rich collection of theological books is supplemented by an extensive collection of works on medieval history, together with excellent resources in the classics, fine arts, social sciences, and Dutch history. In recent years the Sage Library has joined two large theological library associations, the New York Area Theological Library Association (NYATLA) and the Southeastern Pennsylvania Theological Library Assocation (SEPTLA) which collectively comprise nearly 5,000,000 volumes in theology and related disciplines.[9] In the near future, the seminary library will have a computer terminal for access to major computer research networks, through affiliation with Rutgers University. Two such databases, Research Library Information Network (RLIN) and Ohio College Library Center (OCLC), will connect the seminary with the bibliographical resources of major universities and databases all across the country.

The most significant changes to the physical plant and grounds of the seminary have been a result of the New Brunswick Commitment. The capital funds raised were used to finance the renovations of the library and Zwemer Hall, and the reorientation of the campus. During this decade, however, other improvements and additions to the campus have altered the capacity, usefulness, and beauty of Holy Hill.

The first renovation was to 25 Seminary Place, formerly a residence for unmarried students. The renovation in the elegant home—now the president's home, was completed on January 2, 1974.

In 1977, the seminary purchased the property formerly owned by Dr. and Mrs. John W. Beardslee, Jr., at 93 College Avenue and renovated it for use by unmarried students. In addition, renovations were made during the summer in Zwemer Hall in order to provide more office space, a new board room, and a new seminar room.[10]

In the summer of 1980, the Mission House was renamed the Demarest House and made available for faculty housing. For years the Mission House was assumed to be owned by the General Program Council of the Reformed Church. Research in synod and board minutes revealed that the seminary was in fact the owner of the property.[11]

An unusual addition to the seminary plant was the installation of the carillon to the roof of the seminary chapel. Since the demolition of Hertzog Hall, the twenty-five-bell Dutch carillon, which was given to the seminary after the 1939 New York World's Fair, had been in storage in the seminary garage. It was restored by the van Bergen Foundry and electrified so it could be played from the seminary chapel. On October 8, 1982, it was dedicated and now rings regularly throughout the campus.[12] The seminary designated the carillon a memorial to the late Florence Charavay, a generous benefactress of the seminary whose estate included a bequest of a million dollars to New Brunswick Theological Seminary.

Two important organizations which have contributed greatly to seminary life deserve mention: the Women's Auxiliary and the Alumni Association. The Women's Auxiliary has been soliciting funds and contributing time and energy to improving the quality of life at the seminary. Composed of faculty wives and Reformed Church women from the three eastern synods, the auxiliary meets regularly. It seeks gifts from women's groups at the local congregational level to support improvements to the campus, provides scholarship assistance, and its members serve as hostesses at seminary gatherings. During the past decade, the Women's Auxiliary has provided carpeting for the chapel, for the old and new board rooms, and for faculty offices. Hertzog Hall (the cafeteria) was newly carpeted and paneled, and new curtains were provided for the married student residence (Scudder Hall) and the renovated Zwemer Hall (administration building). In addition, the auxiliary has cared for the public areas in student housing. Annually, the Women's Auxiliary sponsors the Francis D. Beardslee Award for the woman student who exhibits excellence in scholarship and exceptional personal growth.

The Alumni Association of New Brunswick has experienced a new surge of activity during this period in the seminary's history. Thousands of dollars have been raised through the annual Alumni Gift Appeal inaugurated in 1980. The Fall Alumni Convocation and the annual alumni reunion days at commencement have become important dates on the alumni calendar. Each year since 1969 the Alumni Association has honored a distinguished alumni with the A. J. Muste Memorial Award. This award is for faithfulness to the ministry of Jesus Christ and persistence in service. In alternate years the award has been given for contributions to social action and service in the church. The award is in honor of the Rev. A. J. Muste, a pastor, pacifist, community organizer, and civil rights advocate, who labored with exemplary faithfulness.[13]

The life of the institution is made up of many parts: the faculty, administration, staff and students, alumni/ae, members of the women's auxiliary, and the churches who contribute daughters, sons, and money. But there are also those individuals who single out an institution which they respect precisely because of all of the activities of the above. One such person—Florence Charavay—has already been mentioned. As the seminary enters her third century, another generous bequest is being probated—the estate of Margaret Baldwin, which has already added $1,200,000 to the seminary endowment. These gifts, added to those of previous donors, have not only allowed the campus and its facilities to be kept in splendid condition, but have allowed for an endow-

ment of approximately four million dollars in added support to
the work of the school.

The uncertainty which surrounded New Brunswick Seminary
in the late sixties and early seventies has given way to renewed
hope and excitement about the future. The new perspective that
New Brunswick acquired in this decade has made it aware that
it should address seriously the challenge of the urban world.
Along with its traditional orientation, it has realized it should be
committed to the city and provide theological education for women
and men who will "seek the welfare of the city where I have sent
you into exile, and pray to the Lord on its behalf, for in its welfare
you will find your welfare" (Jer. 29:7).

The implementation of this vision for the city does not mean
the elimination of the traditional mission of the seminary—the
training of men and women for ministry in the Reformed Church.
Neither does the institution need to deviate from the Reformed
theological perspective which has been its hallmark to meet the
challenge made by urban theological education. The seminary
must simply listen to the needs of women and men in ministry
in the city and respond creatively as it has in the past decade. Its
viability as an on-going institution may be directly linked to its
ability to respond appropriately to the needs for theological education of the diverse population of the Northeast metropolitan
area. It has become apparent to New Brunswick through its work
in New York that there are a significant number of adults throughout this area seeking serious and quality theological education.
The challenge to equip these adult Christians for the task of ministry is compelling and far-reaching. It is hoped that the new
constituencies enrolling in seminary programs will continue to
find New Brunswick a desirable and congenial seminary to pre-
pare them for Christian ministry, whether full time or part time,
day time or evening, as this institution enters its third century
of theological education.

As the Bible begins with the story of a man and a woman in
a garden, and concludes with a vision of a glorious city, the past
of New Brunswick Seminary is a story of a school arising in the

Dutch garden, but now looking to the city as its focus and destination. There is promise in the future of this historic institution because it is preparing women and men for ministry in an urban world.

The faculty in 1984: (back row) David W. Waanders, Virgil M. Rogers, Paul R. Fries, John W. Beardslee III, E. Earle Ellis; (second row) Benjamin Alicea, Charles J. Wissink, Vernon H. Kooy, D. LeRoy Englehardt; (third row) Wilbur T. Washington, Geore Hunsinger; (front row) Frederick Mold, Jr., Howard G. Hageman, Hugh A. Koops.

Footnotes

Chapter 1

1. *Ecclesiastical Records, State of New York*, Albany, 1902. Vol. IV, p. 2685.
2. *Ibid.*, p. 2740.
3. *Ibid.*, p. 2752.
4. *Ibid.*, p. 2812.
5. *Centennial of the Theological Seminary of the Reformed Church in America*, New York, 1885, p. 69.
6. *A Manual of the Reformed Church in America*, E. T. Corwin, New York, 1902, p. 112.
7. *Rutgers: A Bicentennial History*, R. P. McCormick, New Brunswick, 1966, p. 8.
8. *Acts and Proceedings of the General Synod of the Reformed Protestant Dutch Church in North America*, New York, 1859. Vol. I, pp. 13-14.
9. *Ibid.*, pp. 39-40.
10. *Ibid.*, p. 61.

Chapter 2

1. *Acts and Proceedings of the General Synod of the Reformed Protestant Dutch Church in North America*, New York, 1859. Vol. I, p. 116. Henceforth: *Acts and Proceedings.*
2. *Ibid.*, p. 124.
3. *Ibid.*, p. 125.
4. *Centennial of the Theological Seminary of the Reformed Church in America*, New York, 1885, p. 416.
5. *Ibid.*, p. 417.
6. *Acts and Proceedings.* Vol. I, p. 147.
7. *Ibid.*, p. 242.
8. *Ibid.*, p. 261.
9. *Ibid.*, p. 464 et seq.
10. *Ibid.*, pp. 269-70.
11. *Ibid.*, pp. 334-5, 339-40.
12. *Ibid.*, p. 339.
13. *A Manual of the Reformed Church in America*, E. T. Corwin, New York, 1902, p. 168.
14. *Rutgers: A Bicentennial History*, R. P. McCormick, New Brunswick, 1966, p. 23.

15. *Acts and Proceedings.* Vol. I, p. 363.
16. *Ibid.,* p. 366. The full text of the Covenant is found on pages 365-6.
17. *Ibid.,* p. 378. This letter, pp. 368-78, gives a good summary of the history of theological education in the Reformed Church from the begining to 1807.

An Unscientific Postscript

What was the real reason for the denomination's dalliance with the whole question of theological education for almost twenty-five years? Financial stringency is the answer usually given and there is absolutely no evidence for any other explanation. Jealousies and rivalries, however, lurk behind the scenes and every once in a while show their faces a little more clearly.

It must be remembered that the meeting of 1773 had made a commitment to Queen's College as the ultimate site of the professorate. In the coming years there were many hedgings of the question, but there was a general feeling that sooner or later, New Brunswick would be the site of the theological faculty. For those opposed, whatever could postpone the issue might assist in finding another site for the enterprise.

The New York consistory had never been happy about New Brunswick; in its thinking Queen's College was the private toy of wild-eyed evangelicals of whom it wanted no part. It kept the King's College card as one to be played when necessary, as we have seen. But apart from that, in a professor who was one of its own ministers the New York consistory had the best of both worlds. The cost to them was minimal, but they were on center stage in the matter of ministerial training. They were in no hurry to donate money for any other arrangement, and without their support any arrangement was bound to fail.

Another group dissatisfied with the New Brunswick site consisted of those in the Schenectady area who saw no reason why their young men should travel almost from one end of the church to the other, especially after the Schenectady Academy had become Union College in 1795. The appointment of their minister, Dirck Romeyn, as a full professor in 1797 must have indicated to them that the location of a theological institution in Union College was at least a possibility. Thus, they were in no hurry to support something else.

There remains the vexed question of Solomon Froeligh. In view of his secession in 1822 it would be easy to paint him a villain. That would be unfair, but one cannot help suspecting him of some complicity in the delay. Oddly enough, he and Livingston were both products of the mid-Hudson valley and both were supporters of the American cause; in fact there is a strong belief that they fled north together in 1776. The similarities, however, end just about there. Livingston came from an aristocratic manorial family with one of the great New York names; Froeligh was the son of poor German immigrants who were small farmers. (It would be fascinating to know whether they were ever tenants of the Livingstons.) Livingston was trained at Yale and Utrecht; Froeligh had no college education and his theological training was obtained from Goetschius and Romeyn. Livingston had all the social graces and moved with ease among the well-to-do of the commercial emporium; Froeligh, according to accounts from the time, was pretty much a country bumpkin whose manners "were not highly cultivated." Livingston was a polite Federalist; Froeligh was an ardent Democrat and served as a New Jersey elector for Jefferson in 1800.

There can be no question that the Reformed Church contained far more Froelighs than it did Livingstons. To this must be added the fact that Dr. Froeligh was a skilled preacher in Dutch which also endeared him to many in a time of linguistic strife and transition. His appointment as a theological instructor in 1792 could have come as a surprise to no one.

Froeligh was present (as Dr. Livingston was not) at the synod of 1797 when he and Romeyn were named full professors on an equal footing with Livingston. The wisdom of the choice was evidenced by the report of 1800 that he had more students than both of his colleagues. Imagine the shock in 1804 when he allowed his name to be put in nomination for *permanent* professor, only to be defeated by Livingston. There is no record of the number of votes cast for each man, but it was a bitter experience all the same. And this defeat was followed by another in 1807 when his archenemy, James V. C. Romeyn, was named to the superintendents and Froeligh was not.

Is it not possible that in all these developments since 1797 Dr. Livingston increasingly became the enemy, at least to the extent that the circle which Froeligh influenced in Bergen County withheld any support for the professorate, making a third group in the Reformed Church which could not be counted upon financially? Take out the support of New York, Schenectady, and a large part of Bergen County, acknowledge that in many other areas support was at best lukewarm, and that means that only in the Raritan Valley was there any great enthusiasm for the cause.

What finally tipped the scales must have been Dr. Livingston's personal decision. Sometime in 1806 he must have decided that the time had come for him to go to New Brunswick, or the Covenant of 1807 could never have been adopted. In 1806 he was sixty years old and had been a minister in the New York church for thirty-six years. Quite possibly he felt that it was time for a change, that he was no longer the power in the New York pulpit that he once had been. Whatever his reason, Dr. Livingston must have given the nod sometime in 1806 and so set in motion the train of events that led to the move to New Brunswick.

Chapter 3

1. *Acts and Proceedings*, New York, 1859. Vol. I, pp. 416-7.
2. *Ibid.*, pp. 430-3.
3. *Ibid.*, p. 157.
4. *Centennial of the Theological Seminary of the Reformed Church in America*, New York, 1885, pp. 96-7.
5. *Ibid.*, p. 97.
6. *Ibid.*, p. 98.
7. *Ibid.*, p. 435.

1. *Rutgers: A Bicentennial History*, R. P. McCormick, New Brunswick, 1966, p. 41.
2. *Ibid.*, p. 43.
3. *Acts and Proceedings*, New York, 1831. Vol. III, p. 44.
4. *Ibid.*, p. 130.
5. *Ibid.*, pp. 142-3.
6. *Ibid.*, p. 320.
7. McCormick, *Rutgers*, p. 46.
8. *Acts and Proceedings*, New York, 1836, Vol. IV, p. 137.
9. *Ibid.*, p. 211.
10. It is impossible 150 years later to identify all of the dynamics involved in the charges against Professor McClelland. Given the fact, however, that this decade was one of almost continual struggle between the forces of Ludlow and Milledoler for control of the seminary and the fact that Milledoler accused McClelland of conspiring with his enemies, the following seems at least a possible scenario.

    Since most of the activity in the struggle came from the Ludlow faction, it seems possible that the "ultras" persuaded the Classis of New Brunswick, an easy move, to bring the complaint as a diversionary measure, hoping to deflect attention from their own problems and to embarrass their opponents.

    Since Ludlow was present at the synod of 1834 as a delegate from the Classis of Albany and had been named chairman of the Committee of Professorate, he was able to get himself named as chairman of the special committee to investigate the charges. Realizing that his friend McClelland had said some injudicious things for which he could be in deep trouble, Ludlow worked out the compromise of condemning the sermon while reaffirming the person. In this way, nobody lost and nobody won.
11. The experience of New Brunswick in this regard was no different from that of American evangelical Protestantism generally. Page Smith in his volume *The Nation Comes of Age* (New York, 1981) records it in this way.

> The time was ripe for the conversion of a vast number of heathens. The board [the American Board of Commissioners for Foreign Missions with which the Reformed Church at this time cooperated] decided to direct its activities to four fields: . . . It was under this general plan that a mission had been established in Bombay in 1813, in Ceylon in 1816, in the Sandwich Islands in 1820, on the Guinea Coast of Africa in 1833, Sumatra and Borneo a year later . . . [It was with this last extension that New Brunswick volunteers became involved.]
>
> . . . In all these efforts women played a central part, both as fund raisers to sustain missions and as the wives of missionaries who often established schools for native children and shared the tasks of their husbands. (pp. 542-3)

12. *Acts and Proceedings*, New York, 1841, Vol. V, pp. 131-2.
13. *Centennial of the Theological Seminary of the Reformed Church in America*, New York, 1885, p. 449.

Chapter 5

1. *Centennial of the Theological Seminary*, New York, 1885, p. 446.
2. *Acts and Proceedings*, New York, 1846, Vol. VI, p. 490.
3. *Ibid.*, Vol. VII, pp. 191-2.
4. *Ibid.*, Vol. IX, p. 9.
5. *Ibid.*, p. 339.
6. *Ibid.*, p. 559.
7. *Rutgers: A Bicentennial History*, R. P. McCormick, New Brunswick, 1966, p. 86.

Chapter 6

1. *Brooklyn . . . And How it Got that Way*, David W. McCullough, New York, 1982, p. 34.
2. *Acts and Proceedings*, New York, 1865. Vol. X, pp. 625-26.
3. It is impossible to say in what kind of oil stocks Dr. Smith had invested his funds. It seems possible, however, that it was in kerosene which began to be manufactured in Brooklyn in about 1854. Its instant popularity soon disappeared when it was discovered that it had an extremely high combustible point. (See McCullough, *op. cit.*, pp. 40-41.)
4. The fire company in New Baltimore is still known as the J. A. H. Cornell Fire Company because of his generous donations to it. Probably this is one of the few fire companies in the United States named for a Reformed Church minister.
5. *Acts and Proceedings*, 1869, p. 646. After Volume X, the *Acts and Proceedings* no longer have a volume number on the title page. Further, in 1868 the General Synod met not in New York, but in Hudson, New York, and thereafter the place of meeting varies, albeit the *Acts and Proceedings* continue to bear the New York address of the Board of Publication. For purposes of bibliographical reference it seems proper to henceforth identify the *Acts and Proceedings* by short title, year, and page reference.
6. The first two houses built in 1866-7 were on the College Avenue side of the property—Dr. De Witt's house, now the president's house, and Dr. Woodbridge's which is no longer standing. The house on the George Street side of the property was occupied by Dr. Demarest in 1868.
7. *Acts and Proceedings*, 1868, p. 372.
8. Those who remember the old Suydam Hall gymnasium often comment how unsuitable it was for basketball games because of the supporting columns. When the building was erected, basketball had not been in-

vented. Suydam intended the room to be used for gymnastics, wrestling, tumbling, weight lifting, etc., for which it was admirably suited.

9. A full record of the celebration with the texts of all the addresses may be found in *Centennial of the Theological Seminary*, New York, 1885.
10. *Acts and Proceedings*, 1884, pp. 537-540.

Chapter 7

1. *Centennial of the Theological Seminary of the Reformed Church in America*, New York, 1885, pp. 162-3.
2. *Ibid.*, pp. 227-8.
3. *Ibid.*, p. 163.
4. *Acts and Proceedings*, 1886, p. 63.
5. *The Golden Milestone*, James Cantine and Samuel Zwemer, New York, 1939, pp. 18-19.
6. *Ibid.*, p. 29.
7. *Acts and Proceedings*, 1898, p. 95.
8. The writer remembers the late Dr. Demarest (who was 92 at the time) telling him that he had spent most of his life on the four corners of Seminary Place. Dr. Demarest grew up in what is now 1 Seminary Place, which was his father's professorial residence. When he joined the New Brunswick faculty in 1901, he moved into 27 Seminary Place (no longer standing). When he became president of Rutgers in 1906, he moved across the street to the Italianate Gothic frame house which was then the president's house. (It has since been moved several doors down Seminary Place.) After his retirement from Rutgers in 1924, Demarest moved to the stone house at the corner of Seminary and George, which had for many years been used as a seminary faculty residence.

Chapter 8

1. *Centennial of the Theological Seminary of the Reformed Church in America*, New York, 1885, p. 165.
2. Cf. *Acts and Proceedings*, 1902, pp. 207-8.
3. The influence of Dr. Meyer in the New Brunswick community is something of which I became aware through conversations with several older ministers who were students in the 1890s.
4. *Thirty-fifth Annual Report of the Standing Committee*, 1904, p. 5. Included in *Acts and Proceedings*, Vol. XX, after p. 913.
5. *Acts and Proceedings*, 1904, p. 659.
6. *Rutgers: A Bicentennial History*, R. P. McCormick, New Brunswick, 1966, p. 142.
7. This story was told to the writer by the late Dr. David Van Strien who identified himself as one of the leaders of the movement.
8. Dr. Berg once said to the writer that he left the seminary faculty because

he was tired of being where he knew the answer to every question and longed to be where he would be asked questions he could not answer!

9. *Acts and Proceedings*, 1922, p. 780.

Chapter 9

1. *Acts and Proceedings*, 1923, pp. 94-111.
2. *Ibid.*, 1923, p. 99.
3. *Ibid.*, 1925, p. 816.
4. *Ibid.*, 1929, p. 55.
5. *Ibid.*, 1930, p. 455.
6. *Ibid.*, 1931, p. 855.
7. *Ibid.*, 1935, p. 46.

Chapter 10

1. *Acts and Proceedings*, 1936, p. 288.
2. *Ibid.*, 1936, pp. 318-9.
3. *Ibid.*, 1938, p. 414.
4. *Ibid.*, 1948, p. 81.
5. *Ibid.*, 1949, p. 71.

Chapter 11

1. *Acts and Proceedings*, 1960, p. 229.
2. *Ibid.*, 1960, p. 230.
3. The loss of Hertzog and Suydam halls is much to be lamented. Your editor was invited by the then president to act as architectural consultant on the building project. When in my reply I urged the preservation of Suydam and Hertzog halls, and suggested as well that state and federal funding for such projects was just beginning, and would probably be available for historic buildings of such note, I received no reply—no further mention of architectural consultation. While we must lament the loss of those two historic buildings, we must also rejoice in the more recent preservation of the historic Gardner A. Sage Library. All friends of New Brunswick must applaud the leadership of President Hageman which enabled the school to keep faith with her architectural past, and her great benefactor, Gardner A. Sage. The Editor.
4. *Acts and Proceedings*, 1969, p. 43.

Chapter 12

1. *Acts and Proceedings*, 1970, p. 27.
2. *Acts and Proceedings*, 1972, p. 25.

1. A complete text of Dr. Hageman's inaugural address can be found in the *Reformed Review*, Vol. 27, No. 2 (Winter 1984), pp. 83-88.
2. Statistics prepared by Hugh Koops and Irene Thomas for joint Faculty/Management Committee meeting, March, 1983, in New Brunswick.
3. *Acts and Proceedings*, 1974, p. 40.
4. The following faculty are eligible for retirement in the first decade of the seminary's third century: Beardslee (church history); Hageman (president); Englehardt (librarian); Kooy (New Testament); Rogers (Old Testament); Mold (vice president); Washington (homiletics).
5. *Acts and Proceedings*, 1978, pp. 199-200.
6. *Ibid.*, 1979, p. 85.
7. During the queen's visit to New York on June 28, 1982, she honored the president of NBTS, Dr. Howard Hageman, by appointing him to the rank of Commander in the Netherlands' Order of Orange-Nassau. The order of Orange-Nassau is an honor bestowed for special services to the monarch, peoples, or country of the Netherlands.
8. During a reception in honor of Her Majesty and Prince Claus in Sage Library, Dr. Hageman, on behalf of the seminary, presented Queen Beatrix with a rare eighteenth-century Dutch-American pamphlet, in a tooled leather case, entitled " 'Ware Vryhet, tot Vrede' Beantavoort" (" 'True Liberty, the Way of Peace' Answered"). Published in New York in 1761, this unique volume written by Domine John Ritzema was important in the "pamphlet war" between leaders of the Dutch church in New York and New Jersey preceding the founding of Rutgers (then Queen's) College in 1766.
9. Brochures are available at Sage Library with information on the associations and member institution libraries.
10. *Acts and Proceedings*, 1977, p. 160.
11. Management Committee Minutes, December 17, 1979.
12. New Brunswick Theological Seminary Newsletter, September, 1980.
13. The recipients of this award were (year of graduation/year of award): Norman Thomas, 44/69; Ray Pontier, 43/70; Robert Dickson, 43/71; Milton Ortquist, 51/72; Lee Kester, 51/73; Irving Decker, 36/74; Donald Pangburn, 59/75; Adrian Tenhor, 63/76; Fred Baungardner, 48/77; Roland Ratmeyer, 63/78; A. Rand Peabody, 71/79; John Hart, 46/80; J. Dean Dykstra, 43/81; William Cameron, 60/82.